+

C000006031

The CheerLeaders &

Vampires In Your Life

Inspiring People to Inspire Themselves

To: Linda
" one of who's Cheerleaders "
All the Best
Elaine ☺

Elaine Kennedy McIvor

Copyright © 2009 by Elaine Kennedy McIvor
ISBN 978-1-4452-3946-0

Elaine Kennedy McIvor asserts the moral right to be identified as the author of this work.

Dedication

I dedicate this book to the biggest CheerLeaders in my life...

To my parents Hugh & Therese Kennedy who have been a constant source of encouragement in my work and to my best friend, fantastic husband and soul mate Derek McIvor.

Contents

I believe in life there are two kinds of people.

The people you connect with and then there's…
The other people!

I've got a name for these two kinds of people.

I call them...

CheerLeaders & Vampires

The CheerLeaders lift you spirits, are enthusiastic, energisers; people who you feel good around.

The Vampires drain your energy and enthusiasm; they are hard work to be around.

Introduction

Thank you for picking up this book. I have put together some ideas that I hope will help you as much as they have helped thousands of other people. If you want, this book can change the way you look at yourself and others, it can change your life forever, if you choose to use it.

Everywhere you go in life you usually come into contact with other people. There are people with whom you make an instant connection, those who challenge, upset or even irritate you, then there are the people who are just there; people who you may think make no particular imprint at all on your life, that is, until you read this book.

The fact is that every interaction you have on a daily basis, (yes every single one), accumulates and each interaction profoundly affects your life - read on and find out more.

Today is the day you are going to become even more aware of the people in your life and the imprint they leave, as well as the effect you have on the life of other people with whom you come into contact. You can take control of all of your interactions and by doing so you can manage your energy, your attitude and even improve your health and stress levels.

You will be amazed at these simple ideas, how effective they can be in your life. By becoming aware of the way you interact, think and deal with people, you can take control of how you feel and respond. You can take control of your interactions simply by the way you stop doing some things and start spending more time doing others, this book will explain how.

I have studied human engineering now for the last twelve years and, like you, I have been a human being all my life! I have immersed myself in the work of the masters, people like Dale Carnegie, Dr Joseph Murphy, Louise Hay, Susan Jeffers, Dr Wayne Dyer, Lynn Grabhorn, Brian Tracy, Gary Craig, Dr Jill Bolte Taylor and Dawson Church, having spent hundreds of thousands of hours reading books, watching and listening to audio programmes. The main thing I attribute this book to is watching, listening to and learning from other people. Human Beings are absolutely amazing! The laboratory of life that is all around us daily - that is where I have learned and practiced the theories that are in this book.

Each time I get an idea, I try it out in my own life and if it works, I share it with other people in my classes, seminars and workshops. In this book I am not teaching you anything, I am simply sharing ideas with you and I ask you to treat it like a buffet; take a bit at a time and try it, use it if you like it and flush it if you don't. Please don't even try to think about trying to take it all in, in one day, or one week or one month, take one thing at a time and practice it, use it when you can and watch and see what happens.

Although I have read a lot of work on self improvement and do believe in positive thinking, I also believe that people can take it to the extremes and verge on becoming a positive pain in the backside! After all, we are all human and have all had days where, we could have felt better. In fact, maybe you've had days when you would just have preferred to stay in bed and pull the covers over your head! (Yes I have had them too - it's just the "stuff of life.") The good news is, if you didn't have bad days you would have nothing to compare the good ones to!

So if you decide to use the theories in this book, you might think about keeping them to yourself, whatever you do, don't become a positive preacher.   Only share "this stuff" with other likeminded people who are interested, not with people who you think need to hear it! (Try the techniques out on these people and it will help you practice, you may be amazed at the results.) After all, it might be like trying to teach a pig to sing, you would only frustrate yourself and annoy the pig.

There is nothing new in this book, these ideas are ageless. You are probably aware of many of them, but you've maybe just filed them at back of your brain. This book will serve to bring them to the front of your filing cabinet and possibly shine a new light or breathe some new air into old ideas.

When you take some of these ideas that I am sharing with you in this book and you use or even learn them, if appropriate, and if you practice them over and over until they become habits or grooves in your brain (I will talk to you about this idea later) you will be amazed at yourself, and how other people respond to you!

1

CheerLeaders and Vampires

I have got a theory in life about people. I believe that there are two kinds of people; the people you connect with and then... there are the other people!

I have given these people a name; I call them CheerLeaders and Vampires! Yes I know you might have a different name for the latter but let's stick with the polite name for now. May I suggest the next time you meet someone who does challenge you, do not go about telling them they are a Vampire - except if you know them really well and they have read this book.

We live life often surrounded everyday by people, friends, relations, colleagues, acquaintances - people with whom we have a nodding acquaintance, and maybe know to say hello to. We are also surrounded by people whom we don't know; people on buses, trains, planes, in supermarkets, and petrol stations, other drivers on the road, in fact people are just about everywhere.

When we are around people we often get a gut instinct about them, we don't like them, but we don't know why, we just feel uneasy or uncomfortable in their presence. We might not agree with them on much if anything, in fact if we said black, they would probably say white. We may even feel we are on a different wavelength. In extreme cases, it feels like they live on a different planet, never mind wavelength. Everyone I have ever met has experienced this feeling with other people. It is just the stuff of life and the reason I have written this book.

Do you know what I am talking about? Have you got people in your life you get on well and enjoy spending time with, with whom you just hit it off and feel as if you are on the same wavelength as them? Then on the other hand there is the complete opposite scenario. There are the people whom you may avoid like the plague, those who you just do not get on with, you don't like being in their presence, you might feel irritated, uneasy, or even completely uncomfortable around them.

Who are CheerLeaders and Vampires?
I believe they are people, those who surround us every day of our lives, some you notice others go unnoticed, that is until now.

What is a CheerLeader?
You know what a CheerLeader is I am sure; it's someone who stands on the edge of a game and shouts words of enthusiasm, support and encouragement to the participants. Well, I believe a life CheerLeader is just the same; it is someone who stands on the edge of your life who inspires, nurtures, encourages you, someone who just lifts your spirits, and someone who is good to be around. Time probably disappears when you are with them. In short, it's someone who lights up the room when they walk in.

What about a Vampire?
I am sure that you are aware a Vampire is a corpse that rises from the dead to drink and drain the blood from humans. I consider a life Vampire to be someone who drains your enthusiasm, even confidence, who sucks the life energy from

you, someone who is a challenge to have around. In short it's someone who lights up the room when they walk OUT!

Are the wheels starting to turn in your mind right now? Are you thinking of one or two people (or three or four or more) who fit the Vampire description in your life? That's natural; please do yourself a favour though, do try to refrain from verbalising it, I will explain why later.

What about you? How do you think you impact others? Would you say you light up the room when you walk in, or does the room light up when you leave? Are people glad for having been around you? Read on and find more.

2

Who are CheerLeaders and Vampires?

Let me ask you a question. Who have you come into contact with today? Since you opened your eyes this morning, who have you come into contact with? Whose was the first voice you heard or who was the first person you saw today? Was it someone in your bed? (I used to sleep with a Vampire!) A member of your family in your home?

Maybe, it was someone on the radio, or the television? Was it another driver on the road? The postman? The lollipop man/woman? The person from whom you bought your morning paper? The person to whom you answered the telephone? Maybe it was a fellow passenger on the bus, train, plane or what about a work colleague? Maybe it was someone whom you thought about the moment you opened your eyes? Stop reading this page for a moment and think about your day.

How has it left you feeling? Energised or drained?
Did you feel the better for meeting with, speaking to, seeing or hearing that other person? Or would you rather that you had managed to avoid that particular person? Did the connection leave you feeling great, or did it, in fact, have the completely opposite effect?

What about the rest of the time?
Who do you come into contact with day in day out, week in week out, month in, month out, year in year out?

Wherever you go, whatever you do in life, you usually come into contact with other people, because wherever you go, you are there! When you connect with other people, each connection generally has a positive or negative effect on how you feel your energy and emotions. It is very rarely neutral. In fact, people usually interact on automatic pilot and take each connection for granted. We will discuss why this is in more detail later, but for now consider this... I firmly believe:

Every single connection YOU have with another human being impacts on YOUR life!

At this point you may have come to the conclusion that the people closest to you can be your biggest Vampires, like your mum or dad, sister or brother, or your best friend! Relax, you are not alone. This comes up in my sessions all the time. We will talk more about it later in the book, and give you ideas and mechanisms to help you. (It is a true saying; you can choose your friends…)

If someone energises you, how do you know? If someone drains you how do you know? The answer is you know because you can feel it, the way you grit your teeth, the way your heart sinks at the mention of their name, the way the hairs stand up on the back of your neck, the way you seem to stop breathing at the sight of them, the tension you feel in your body. You immediately know by your feelings if you connect with someone or you don't.

What about you? What affect do you think you have on other people? What would you say; do you leave people feeling energised or drained?

When you feel energised around people, do you feel tense and nervous? No. It is usually quite the opposite; when you feel good around others, you are calm and relaxed, feel in control and your true personality usually shines through, you are more like your true self.

3

How to Recognise Your CheerLeaders and Vampires

I am sure you already know how to recognise them but read on. There are maybe some lurking around in your life that you didn't know about and you don't want them pouncing on you when you are not looking. Let's look at the Vampires in more detail.

Where do the Vampires live? Do they sleep in coffins and only come out at night? They lurk everywhere day and night. If you are full of energy, chances are they will prey on you and suck you dry!

What do they look like?
Smug... like, oh yes I told you so! Well, this says it all. Sometimes it just takes a look from one and you're drained! (If looks could kill...?) The challenge is that you may not be able to tell they are a Vampire by just looking at them. Although with some people they don't even need to speak. You can tell by the expression they wear on their face - this alone may suck you dry or the fact that you can hear them breathing challenges you even when they are happy, you wouldn't know it as they never tell their face.

What do they sound like?
Yep, you're right again. They never seem to be full of the joys. Are they condescending or patronizing? They all sound

different, when you get into conversation with one of yours, you will know right away, by the way the hairs stand up on the back of your neck during the conversation (in extreme cases they don't even need to open their mouth for this to happen, it occurs by simply having one present) or by the big hole you feel in the pit of your stomach, or the overwhelming urge to yawn, or by the irritated feeling that takes over you, during your connection or rather misconnection with this person.

After coming up with the theory of CheerLeaders and Vampires, I realised that I used to sleep with one. Yes, you're right - there was one in my bed! How did I know? Well, in the morning when I used to wake up feeling great, looking forward to the day ahead, I suddenly heard this long low moan from the other side of the bed; that signalled first of all there was a Vampire present, and, of course, that the Vampire had woken up, and was definitely not happy that it was daylight, which meant he had to go to work (which at the time to put it politely really challenged him).

So he would moan and groan and go on about "having to get up." Oh No! Not you too! You've got one in your bed too? Don't worry - just read on to find out if you should take some garlic to bed with you! The Vampire I used to sleep with is now my husband. He is my best friend and biggest CheerLeader, I am sure over the years he too was sleeping with a Vampire, yes you guessed right... me!

Where do you find them?
You can find them anywhere. Wherever you go, when you come into contact with other people and you feel challenged in some way. You will be even more aware of them now, as you read on you will understand how this awareness is beneficial to you.

12

Have you ever gone into a shop to buy a newspaper and the person who is serving you is talking to their colleague? Or maybe you have gone to the supermarket and the check-out operator is talking across the aisle to her colleague? How do you feel when that happens to you? Ignored, invisible, not important, angry or frustrated?

Maybe you have stood up in front of a group to do a presentation and there is someone in the room who is staring out of the window and not paying attention to what you are saying. Maybe you have had a meeting with some colleagues, and one of them makes no eye contact with you, or when you open your mouth to make a comment they speak over the top of you.

Every day in every way you come into contact with other people who may act in ways that I have described above. As you read on you will begin to understand why the Vampires display this kind of behaviour and why you feel drained around them. You will learn ways to manage your energy in the face of someone who has a Vampire effect on you.

4

Vampire Varieties

Here are some particular kinds of Vampire varieties which I
have come across on my journey through life so far.

The Whinge (Mr or Mrs Moan)
This is the kind of Vampire whose voice sounds like a high
pitch whine; their cup is always half empty, it is never half full.
They spend their life moaning about this and complaining about
that. In fact, they are under the impression they actually have a
gift for identifying what is wrong in life, (or your life) with
situations and with people. They would never think of looking
for what is right. You can often see the black cloud above their
head, or the hunch in their shoulders from where the world is
situated, or even the drop in their posture from the heavy
luggage that they constantly carry around with them.

The Materialist
This person is so draining. They talk about themselves all the
time; what they've got, how many they have, how much it cost,
where they've been, where they are going. When they meet you
the first thing they do is check you out… you know, they look
you up and down. It's never done discreetly, it is always
blatantly obvious.

They need to be the centre of the conversation. I remember
having a party many years ago and there was a materialist
present. What happened was she was one of the first to arrive
with another couple. For the first hour or so she was the centre

of attention. As the other guests started to arrive the attention slowly came off her. Before much longer she actually announced she was going home and promptly left the party.

These kinds of people wear an air of superiority about them and often talk down to other people. In fact they talk, talk, and talk about themselves all the time and they just are not interested in you. Chances are if they do ask you how you are, even if you said you had been off work with a broken leg, they would have broken theirs too, but of course, theirs' would have been broken in two or three places, not just one!

The Pessimist
This one appears so often. They are always focusing on the worst, looking for what could go wrong, always negative about anything different or new you attempt to do. When you come up with a new idea they will find a reason why it won't work. Chances are, they live their life out of habit, just doing the same old same old and not daring to do anything different.

The Humiliator (Mr & Mrs Mega Mouth)
This person delights in making a fool of other people. He listens to conversations waiting for you to slip up then promptly highlights your mistake or makes fun of you in a loud voice for everyone to hear.

Intimidator (Mr or Mrs "I wouldn't do it like that")
These people probe questions into other people's world with the intention of finding something wrong. Once they do, they then criticize the aspects of the other person's life; you end up being drained of energy because you then judge yourself by what he may be thinking. They are constantly telling you what you need to do to sort out your life. People often can become withdrawn

15

in the company of intimidator Vampires, they hold back on conversation for fear of being criticised.

(Mr or Mrs Me)

These people talk about themselves all the time. It doesn't matter what you are talking about, they always get the conversation back round to them and their life. I love me... who do you love.

The Victim (Mr or Mrs "It's really your fault")

Victims love people to be pouring energy into them. Nothing is ever their fault; they are always looking to point the finger at other people. They constantly talk about all the bad things that happen to them. Sometimes they insinuate that it is your fault. Have you been around someone who you feel is encouraging you to feel guilty? They infer that you are not doing enough to help them. They constantly talk about how the world owes them.

Worry Wart

This person is addicted to worrying. They are always looking for the next thing to worry about, and if that situation is sorted then their answer is "Well I suppose that is one less thing for me to worry about!" They get themselves into to a complete state of stress and anxiety with constantly finding things to worry about.

The Hypochondriac

I couldn't miss this one out now, could I? This person needs no introduction or explanation really. People who always have something wrong with them, and are happy to explain to you what it nearly was.

The Little Hitler – Dominator

This person could not be more direct if they tried. Something like a bull in a china shop might come to mind. They are very direct and to the point; if something is on their mind, there are no holds barred - they just come right out and say it. They are not particularly good at listening but very good at telling you what's to be done and that it's your job to do it. They are - absolutely brilliant at being confrontational.

The Machine Gun

This person just loves to talk and talk. In fact they talk at 60000 words per hour with gusts up to 80000. They just talk all the time; they think when you are talking and you take a breath, that this is their cue to jump right on in there and fill the gap! They love being the centre of attention and are so enthusiastic sometimes it's painful. They often need to remember to take their foot off the exaggerator, so focusing for this person is difficult as they would rather talk than listen and concentrate.

The Fencer

That's what this person does, just sits on the fence. If you ask them a question like "Do you want a cup of tea," chances are they might say to you, "I don't know, what do you think?" They are very sensitive and it can be like walking on eggshells around them trying to be careful what you say. When it comes to change, if you want to change anything, don't ask them - they will tell you to keep things just the way they are.

Mr Perfect

The perfectionist, everything must be perfect because they are perfect, have you dotted your I's and crossed your T's? If not they will want to know why. They analyse absolutely everything. In fact sometimes they can appear really stuck up and aloof, because they are overly critical of what you do and

17

how you do it. There can be no grey areas here - everything has got to have an answer to their question and if not, they want to know "Why not?" In fact they are rarely wrong!

The Everyday Vampire

Now you may be wondering about this type. This is the Vampire you will meet the most. They may not quite fit any of the descriptions above, but you just feel irritated, or uncomfortable or even ignored around them.

Let me give you an example. I was shopping in a supermarket one morning, it doesn't matter which one, it was just more or less immediately after opening time. The staff were still packing shelves and getting organised. There were not too many customers around because it was so early. I had picked up a couple of things that I needed and was approaching the check out with my shopping basket. The operator at my check out was having a conversation across the aisle in front of me with her colleague. They were talking about a wedding that one of them was going to.

Now as I approached and put my shopping on the conveyer belt I thought, "I will be acknowledged in a minute I am sure. They will stop chatting." But no, they carried on, as I walked to the bottom of the lane to pay, they carried on talking. In fact, I might have well been invisible even although I had to walk through the conversation, they carried on. My check out operator processed my goods on automatic pilot while still deep in conversation with her colleague. Then I handed over my debit card, as she put it in the machine, she took a breath from her conversation with her colleague and said "Cash back?"

Well as you can imagine I felt completely ignored, invisible almost, so I was slightly annoyed. What should I do, to make

18

her aware that she was ignoring me and it was rude? Well, I looked up in surprise and said "Oh! Are you talking to me?" The look on her face was enough. She understood right away that she had been rude and shown no customer service, never mind manners. Now at that moment I really thought about giving her a piece of my mind, or going to the customer service desk to complain about the lack of manners. Then I thought, no, I did not want to give the situation any more of my time, effort, energy or space in my head and promptly left the shop.

The Vampires that you meet every day in work, at meetings, while shopping, while travelling or just generally going about your day, are people who lack the fundamental basics in life; people skills. They lack the ability to make eye contact, to acknowledge you. They talk over the top of you. You might feel ignored they don't know the meaning of the word "listen." They have run out of smiles completely and the main reason for this is that they are acting on "automatic pilot." These people are the ones who zap your energy the most. In fact, sometimes you don't even know your energy is being drained until you get to the end of the day and you are completely exhausted. There are various reasons people display particular traits, and behaviour. Later I will give you some coping mechanisms that I use to manage this kind of interaction, to help stop you having an energy leak.

Before we leave this section, would you recognise yourself here? Are there days when you moan and complain, or are you always telling others what you have and how much it cost? Do you talk over the top of other people, or if something goes wrong, are you the one who is always first to point the finger or find someone else to blame? Are you the person who chooses to focus on what is wrong instead of what is right about other people? Do you always find something to worry about? When you go through your day do you pay attention to the people you are with, no matter who they are?

Can my CheerLeaders sometimes be my Vampires?

Of course anyone can be a Vampire, by having a draining effect on you. Often in my sessions people will say "Elaine I know this is a terrible thing to say but it's my mother who is my biggest Vampire" or "my father", or "my sister", or "my husband." If you are around others who challenge, irritate, upset, frustrate you or in some way cause you to experience some sort of negative feeling in your body which is disrupting how you feel, then it is perfectly natural that this produces a Vampire effect on you. It is just the stuff of life, I will show you how to handle that feeling and what to do to overcome it and not carry it around with you, affecting your day or your life.

5

Who is Your Biggest Vampire?

Why am I asking you this question? You have no idea the number of times I have been asked in sessions "Elaine, what if your biggest Vampire is yourself?" That is why I am asking you the question now.

I always ask this question in my sessions, and often the same answer comes up time and again. It could be you! Most people recognise this. We are all good at self talk, criticising, complaining, and stressing ourselves out. Some people are more guilty of it than others, but everyone does it to some extent.

After reading about Vampires previously, you may already be thinking of people in your life who have a draining effect on you, leave you exhausted or irritated because they are always right, or always complaining, or constantly looking for someone to blame etc.

No-one is superhuman and it is completely natural to talk about yourself; people are their own favourite topic of conversation, admittedly some more than others. However, reading this may help you to become more aware of yourself. Listen to yourself in conversation with others. What are you talking about? Do you listen or do you take over the conversation? Do you tell others what to do and how to do it?

After reading this book you will become more aware of yourself and others. I would encourage you to read it time and again; it is incredible how quickly the human mind files information. I

21

constantly read and feed my mind with information. It's amazing that you never forget to feed your body to keep up your energy levels, but feeding your mind with good information can prove to be even more important to your health than you could possibly imagine.

Everyone exists to a large extent on "automatic." Your subconscious mind really takes care of you; you don't need to think about breathing, blinking, or scratching your nose. You do it automatically. Your heart beats, the blood gets pumped round your body, you digest food. Thankfully, it is all done naturally without you having to think about it.

That is what happens with our day to day life. Most people go into their day and their interactions with others without giving it a second thought. They just go with the flow. You greet people the way you always have, you answer the phone the way you have always done, you like who you like, you avoid who you don't if you possibly can, and your life goes on. You are with you every second of every minute of every day.

How is your life? Are you happy, do you feel good, do you enjoy your life, do you look forward to each new day, or is it an effort to get out of bed? Are you automatically happy most of the time? Are you automatically miserable most of the time? Are you, your biggest Vampire?

What are you consistently saying to yourself? What do you believe about yourself? Are you in control of yourself and your life, are you supporting and encouraging yourself, or are you sabotaging your own success by what you say when you talk to yourself?

Take control of your inner Vampire and stop draining away your own energy. This is your life; you have a right to live it to the full. I will give you some strategies to deal with your inner Vampire further on in the book, but being aware that you might be your biggest Vampire is a fantastic start because the start of any process of change is awareness. When you are aware you are doing something then you can begin to make different choices.

Every single interaction you have accumulates and profoundly affects you.

You are with you all the time. Self talk is interaction with yourself. Everyone has a CheerLeader and Vampire in their head.

6

CheerLeader Traits

So far we have looked at the Vampire traits and varieties. Now we are going to look at the opposite, the CheerLeaders.

How do you recognise a CheerLeader?
I really do believe that on a rare occasion you meet an individual who changes your perception of the world and maybe your perception of yourself. It might be someone that you know or on the other hand it may be a complete stranger. Life is so exciting. You just never know from day to day who is going to make an appearance in the story of your life.

What do they look like?
Do they run around with pom poms? No, of course they don't. In fact they may be challenging to find. Do they walk about with a fixed smiled on their face? Probably not, but the chances are they may look much more approachable than "the other people" - you know, those who carry the world on their back affecting their posture. Although everyone is different it might not be until you start speaking with them that you realise the kind of person they are. Jack Black, the author and founder of "The MindStore System", declares that: "You can tell someone's attitude to life just by listening to them speak." I totally agree.

What do they sound like?
This is an interesting one because when you are in contact with these people you may be the one doing the talking as they are

great listeners. On the other hand, if they are talking, chances are they are probably talking to you about you, or giving you some sound information or encouragement. When you come into contact with one you will know by the gut feeling you get and the instant connection you feel to them.

Why do you feel good around them?
CheerLeaders have the ability to give of themselves. They transmit positive energy and they create an incredible ripple effect. I like to compare it to a wizard or an angel, sprinkling happy dust in their path which affects everyone they meet. (Maybe a bit farfetched but hey, that's MY STUFF... I'm visual for goodness sake, I can't help it!)

When you are around someone like this you just feel good; you feel listened to, heard, important, acknowledged, appreciated, worthwhile. In fact, I have heard it said, in one of my workshops that you can actually feel "Drunk on Life!"

Where can you find them?
Does "needle in a haystack" come to mind? There may be a lot of people in your life who you connect with, who you feel that you are on the same wavelength as, but how many of them do you feel are a huge source of energy to you? When you are with them, it is a "two way" conversation. You can trust them to talk about "your stuff", and not feel that you are dumping on them because you both have a similar outlook and you look for coping mechanism. You listen to one another, help one another, understand one another.

In contrast to the traits of the Vampires such as "the Whinge", "the Materialist", "the Humiliator", "the Intimidator", "the Victim", you don't tend to hear these people that I call "CheerLeaders" complaining much or talking about themselves in a materialistic way. They don't make a fool of others; they may laugh with you but not "at you". They do not intimidate others and don't know the meaning of the word "victim". Okay, so they sound like perfect angels; let's face it, we are all human but these people have taken control of their life and are very particular about whom they choose to share "THEIR STUFF" with. For now, let's look further into your life and your "Stuff".

Before we leave this section, would you recognise yourself here? Would you say you are approachable? Are you a listener or a talker? Do you listen to people with your eyes and your ears when you are talking to them? Are you a source of energy and enthusiasm to others, do you encourage people, always catch them doing something right? Do you look for the solution to the situation instead of the problem in it? Are people drunk on life around you? Do you build other people up giving them confidence in who they are?

"Life takes on a new meaning when you become a source of encouragement to others and associate with people who encourage you."

-Elaine Kennedy McIvor

7

What Affects Your Energy?

Wherever you go in life, you are there! Someone said this to me a long time ago. I cannot recall who it was but I found it amusing. I like it, so I use it now too.

Life is huge. The quality of your life is so important. This is your life. Today might be the beginning of a new fresh page, new chapter, or perhaps even a brand new book. Your life is a blank canvas and you are the artist, the author, the creator. The quality of your energy is the key to the quality of your health, well being, and happiness.

Since coming up with the theory of CheerLeaders and Vampires, I have been more and more aware of how I feel and what affects my energy. Now I want to show you something that I have developed that I base all my work around. It is called "The CheerLeader and Vampire Circle of Energy." I have always worked in what I like to call the "Feel Good Industry", helping people to feel good about themselves. Let me explain in a little more detail.

I worked in Local Government from leaving school at sixteen until I was in my early thirties. This is when I first started to feed my brain by reading and began to realise that I could take control of my life and that I didn't need to stay there until I retired. For some people this is what they want and I respect that, but I always knew it was not what I wanted.

I went to America to train as a colourist. America is one of my favourite places, and I was actually in tears when I left the country the first time. I just loved it so much. I really enjoyed working with colour and would go out and talk to groups on how to use colour to get "The Feel Good Factor." From there I decided to train in Colour Therapeutics, and studied with The Holistic Design Institute. Colour therapeutics is the use of colour in your environment, at home, at work, and in the garden too.

I would do Colour Consultations and people could really see the difference in finding their own unique colours; for wardrobe, hair and makeup made, to help their look and (more importantly) improve their confidence. I designed "Days of Inspiration" for what I called "Real Woman", enlisting the help of expert friends in the field of makeup, hair and clothing. I also used feel good music which added to the fantastic atmosphere.

From there I worked as a class manager for "Scottish Slimmers", Scotland's own leading weight management company. This work really took me inside the mind of people and helped me understand how their image affected their confidence. It taught me that making simple changes to food choices, completely changed people's lives for the better. It changed their look, improved their health and well being and that was just for starters. Amazing things can happen when you become aware of what you are feeding your body. I saw people change from week to week before my very eyes, food really does affect your energy in a big way.

So I also began to study how food really can influence the mood. The Scottish Slimmers way of eating is all about helping people bring balance when it comes to food. No food is banned, it simply is a very healthy way of eating which I use and I highly recommend it.

A fantastic book which I constantly refer to is "SuperFoods to Boost Your Mood" by Alexandra Massey with Anita Bean. This is the book that I recommend to my clients who have challenges with depression, fatigue and stress. What you feed your body really does impact your life; it impacts your mind just as much as your body.

A fantastic chapter of my life was when I went to work for Scotland's own Jack Black who developed "MindStore." When I worked in local government I had heard people saying "It only works!"- a phrase coined by Jack himself. I bought his book and read it. I really began to put the principles to use in my life. Then through work I actually got the opportunity to go and experience a MindStore course for myself. It was amazing. I highly recommend it. This course taught me to think positively, use "whole brain" thinking and achieve goals. At that time as I was really interested in positive attitude and energy, I decided that if this stuff really works', I would programme myself to work with MindStore, and I decided that Jack Black himself would invite me to work with his organisation. I used the tools that I was taught, consistently.

Within two years I was a member of Jack's MindStore team. Lots of incredible things happened in those two years, and to top it all when Jack found out I was interested in being a member of staff he called me up and said he would be delighted to have me on board, so all the tools he taught me worked. I was a product of the "MindStore System" and used to love chatting to the fantastic members. Those were very interesting years of my life and I learned a lot. I met amazing people, some of whom I am still in touch with today. That part of my life I spent around like- minded people, and most of the time I had my head stuck in books as I just adored feeding my mind with "brain food."

I have to say that Jack helped me a lot - on one occasion he invited me to speak to his audience at Glasgow's Royal Concert Hall, to an amazing 1300 people at a Mind Store for Life event. What an experience! Jack knew I was going to talk about the corporate side of MindStore, but he did not know what I was going to say. He always "trusted the process." I spoke for about ten minutes. The energy in the room was amazing and speaking to a MindStore audience of like-minded and open-minded people was just incredible.

That part of my life really helped me to appreciate what it was like to associate with like-minded people and to understand the influence that the mind can have on the body and on life itself. It also gave me the opportunity to be exposed to all kinds of fantastic reading material as there was always bookshops at the courses. It helped me to realise something too - I was responsible for calling people up after the events to give support and in the following few days people were really buzzing but, like anything, as time went on, their enthusiasm became somewhat diluted. I knew the MindStore tools were great, and they worked (I am living proof) but what I realised was when people went back to "their life", to the people they associated with constantly, if they didn't commit themselves and use the tools, they would fall back to their old habits and ways of thinking. This really helped me realise the impact of outside influences on us, as well as what we feed our brain.

If you want more information on MindStore visit the website www.mindstore.com

So from my life experience I could see a picture developing. I used to write my journal all the time; when I was around people who said something that made me think, I would write it down. I always carried a notebook and pen wherever I went. In fact I still do today, I now write what I call "The Purple Journals" which are my thoughts and life experiences in a journal that is purple in colour. I also used Mind Maps a lot (the brain child of Tony Buzan). By using this kind of method to make notes it all began to fit together and make sense. Look up Tony Buzan - he is the author of many books on Mind Mapping, you will find them useful. I use them a lot when I am presenting. I used to put my thinking down on paper using a Mind Map and eventually I developed what I now call "The CheerLeaders and Vampires Circle of Energy."

So now let's take a look at what I believe influences our energy.

8

The CheerLeaders and Vampires
Circle of Energy©

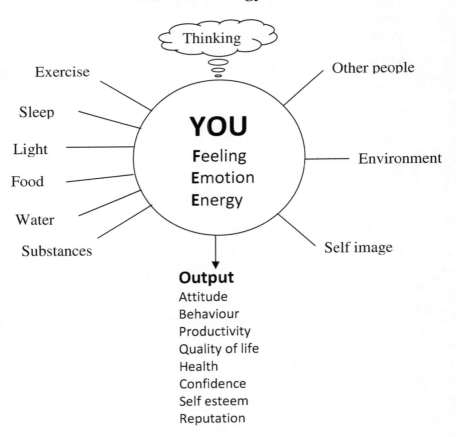

**Every interaction you have accumulates and profoundly
affects your energy and your life.**

The CheerLeader and Vampire Circle of Energy©

Every day you are constantly using, giving and receiving energy to those whom you are with and to what you are doing. You are in the middle of the circle. There are lots of different things which affect how you feel; your energy, your attitude, your behaviour, and your life.

I am sure you are already aware of the more practical things for example:

Light
How much time do you spend out in the daylight?
How much better do you feel on a sunny day? People spend more time stopping for a chat or in the garden when the weather is good. In Scotland it is fabulous when the sun does shine! Some people travel great distances for some sunshine, others live in countries where the sun shines more often. The sun is good for us if we are careful with it. As humans, our bodies are made up of energy (amongst other things) and natural light gives you energy. Daylight is made up of different colours but we see it as white light. The only time we see all the colours in the daylight is when the sun is out and it rains at the same time and a rainbow appears - this shows you all the colours that light is made from. So, getting as much natural light as possible in your home and your environment is good for you, it is energising.

Water
How much water do you drink?
Our bodies and our brain are made up of a high percentage of water. Water is fabulous for flushing toxins out of the body and it can aid weight loss. If you are feeling tired or lethargic, often a glass of water is all you need to refresh your mind and body.

33

Water has incredible healing abilities. Water is energising and if you don't drink a lot of water, I would encourage you to begin your day with a glass of water gently and gradually increase your water intake.

Exercise
When you move your body you are exercising it. When you get out of your bed and walk to the bathroom in the morning, you are exercising. When you brush your teeth you are exercising, when you walk round the shops you are exercising. Exercise should be fun, it should be enjoyed and not be a bind. If it is a bind, if you dread it, you could be draining yourself of energy with negative thinking. There are fabulous gyms, classes, trainers, teachers out there, so go and find someone who will show you the joy of exercise. The more energy you use, the more energy you have. Exercise releases feel good chemicals in the brain.

Sleep
Sleep is a great way of refuelling and healing the body. Sleep is important to us. If you are having challenges sleeping because you are worried about something, or maybe you have a young family at home, or are caring for someone who has a health challenge and you don't get a lot of sleep, then of course it does affect your energy, and how you are feeling. When you can, take 5 or 10 minutes here and there and just sit with your eyes closed and relax, it can help. I often do this throughout the day, and feel so much better after it.

Food
Food can affect your mood and your energy big time, often times people don't realise just how much impact food really has. Following a healthy eating routine is very important. The kind

of food and the amount of food you eat impacts your energy and your mood.

Substances
I have included substances in this section. This covers anything else that you choose to put into your body to change the way you feel. It may be drugs, alcohol, cigarettes. I would also say medication too; you may have been prescribed medication to help you get back to health.

The Other Stuff
Now I want to take a look at the other things that affect how you feel, things that you may not have considered much in the past. I hope reading this will raise your awareness.

Environment
What surrounds you daily in your environment? Your environment can have a huge impact; where you spend your time, be it at home, at work or elsewhere.

Self Image
What do you see when you look in the mirror? How do you see yourself, how do you feel about who you are? How you look, what you wear, your clothes, your hair, your makeup, your perfume or aftershave, more or less everything you choose to use on your body can influence your energy levels and how you feel about yourself. Every day you give yourself a dose of colour energy by the garments you wear and the food you eat.

How are you feeling right now?
If I was to call you right now and ask you that question what would your answer be? So imagine the phone is ringing and you pick it up and I ask you right now "How are you?" What would your reply be? Take a moment to think about it. Would

your reply be "Well, yes I am okay" or "I am fine", or "Not bad thanks?" Or would your reply be… "I am absolutely brilliant," "I feel fabulous", "Just great?" Only you know the answer. Are you feeling great? Or could you be feeling better?

If you are feeling good, why are you feeling good? What are you thinking about, where are you, what are you wearing, who are you with, what are the factors that have given you that feeling at this moment?

If you could be feeling better, what are you thinking about, who are you with, what are you wearing, where are you, what are the factors that are influencing how you are feeling right now?

The more you become aware of your energy and what influences it, the more you can manage to take control of yourself and your life. This book will serve to raise your awareness and give you coping mechanisms for managing and improving the quality of your energy and give you ideas to feed your brain as well as your body. With practice and repetition you really can feel better. These are the three key principles in this book:

1. **Raise Your Awareness**
2. **Feed Your Brain**
3. **Practice and Repeat**

Thinking and Other People
How you are feeling right now is dependent on so many different factors, but for the purposes of this book I want to focus on two factors that I really believe can influence your energy the most and they are "Thinking" and "Other People."

I am sure that, generally speaking, what you have read in this chapter makes perfect sense; if you want to feel good and be healthy, eating properly, getting the right amount of sleep, taking regular exercise, drinking water, this is all very important.

There is excellent information available out there on, for example, what you wear improves your look and how you feel. Also as your home is your third skin, it is important that you enjoy being there. The environment that you spend your time in at work or at home is important too, as we have discussed.

I truly believe that the two things that can influence how you feel in a big way are "Thinking and Other People." The next part of the book goes on to explain why you may connect with some people and not with others and what you can do to help yourself manage your energy, how the interactions you have had with other people in the past and in the present may be shaping your life, your attitude and your energy today.

The information I am giving you is a result of my own life experience, my own observations and what I did personally to move forward.

I believe that in life "Every interaction you have accumulates and affects you, your life and your energy."

9

The Energy Exchange

As I said at the beginning of the book, there are people you connect with and then there are the other people. When you come into contact with other people you immediately know whether or not you connect, because your instinct tells you, you can feel it. An energy exchange takes place when you come into contact with other people. Your body is a field of warm energy.

Right now if you are sitting down reading this book, and after a while you get up and someone takes your seat, it would probably be warm wouldn't it? Have you ever got on a train or bus and sat down and felt that the seat was still warm from the previous person, or rolled over to the other side of the bed when someone has just got out, feeling the body heat they left behind? This is just energy. Energy is leaving your body all the time.

Have you ever watched something on TV (it is usually on the police programmes) where they are maybe chasing someone at night, and they are using an infra red camera so they will be able to detect the person's body heat and it shows up on the camera in red? That is energy.

Have you ever gone to a party at someone's house and they've just had an argument and you are not supposed to know? But you just know they have, you can instinctively tell because you can feel it, it's like you could cut the atmosphere with a knife, that is energy.

You are made up of energy. When you come into contact with other people there is an energy exchange; a silent energy exchange that happens. You are transmitting energy information all the time and so are other people.

FAB

Facial Expression – The way you look at people
Attitude – The way you are with other people
Body Language – Your posture

The more people you come into contact with the greater the exchange of energy and the more your energy can be affected. Have you ever gone out for a day's shopping and come back feeling drained? Maybe you felt the need to go for a coffee to make yourself feel better and you have a wee treat too, just to give you an energy boost?

When you go to an event where there are hundreds or thousands of people the energy or atmosphere can be incredible. Maybe you've been to a concert to see your favourite band, or a football or rugby game to support your team, and the atmosphere or energy in the place is just electric. You know because you can feel all the energy emanating from people. When groups of people come together their energy charges the atmosphere.

As a human being you are constantly giving off or transmitting energy, exchanging energy, or losing energy. You know when you energy is low because you can feel it; you can become tired, irritable, hungry, stressed or in extreme cases ill.

When you feel that your energy is low, you know that you need to do something to change the way you feel. You might feel the need to sleep, have a meal, go out for a walk, or maybe you feel the need to exercise, meditate, listen to music. Whatever it is that you do helps fill your energy up again and helps you feel better.

When your energy levels are low, you are less resilient; it can affect you in so many ways. The more you become aware of your energy, the more you can do to protect it, maximise it, and channel it to improve every area of your life.

Later on in the book I am going to show you a very simple exercise to help you manage your energy and give yourself a power surge.

Every single interaction you have accumulates and profoundly affects you and your energy.

10

Dr Jill Bolte Taylor & the Energy Exchange

I want to tell you a story about an amazing woman called Dr Jill Bolte Taylor, who is a brain scientist and suffered a stroke at the age of 37 damaging the left side of her brain. For a time Dr Taylor lived in her right brain.

I came across this incredible person, some people would say, quite by accident, or coincidence, or by the law of attraction, (which I will go on to talk about later in the CheerLeaders and Vampires series of books). I believe people come into your life for a reason, a season or a lifetime.

This is what happened; one Saturday evening I was home alone, which was quite unusual for me as Derek and I usually spend our Saturday evenings relaxing, listening to music away from the TV. Having spent most of the day reading, I decided to take a break and put on some TV, so I switched on The Oprah Winfrey Show. Dr Oz was on with Oprah whom I recognised, along with another other woman whom I didn't know.

All I heard coming from the TV even before I settled down after switching it on was **"I couldn't communicate verbally, I could only feel peoples presence by their energy"** and, of course, my ears perked up. The woman went on to say that even although she was in hospital with nurses and doctors, with certain people she did not feel safe, she felt exhausted and drained in their presence, with others she felt instantly safe in their care.

I listened intently and realised that the person who was speaking was Dr Jill Bolte Taylor, a brain scientist, who herself had experienced damage to her brain. When she was 37 years old, she experienced a massive stroke when a blood vessel exploded in the left side of her brain, leaving her unable to walk, talk, read, write or recall any of her life, all within the space of a few hours.

I ordered the book "My Stroke of Insight" instantly online, it arrived within a few days and from the moment I opened it I was glued. I sat there and (as I do with all my books,) with my pen, underlined lots of different parts so I could review those particular parts at a later date when I was re-reading the book. I would recommend that everyone read this book. It is phenomenal.

At this time I was writing this book about CheerLeaders and Vampires, about the energy exchange that happens when you come into contact with others. Here, in front of my eyes, was a fantastic brain scientist who had lost the power of the left logical side of her brain, who described her left brain "going off line for a time." She lived in her right brain and describes her own experience beautifully.

She experienced people "as concentrated packages of energy", she described the doctors and nurses as she saw them "a massive conglomeration of powerful beams of energy that came and went."

As Dr Taylor shifted to living in her right brain, she became very sensitive and empathetic to what other people felt; she began to pay very close attention to how other people's energy affected her. What she said in her book was "I realised that some people brought me energy while others took it away."

Here is a brain scientist who understands the power of the brain, who experienced her left brain shutting down, living in her right brain and experienced people as CheerLeaders and Vampires with her energy! Read Dr Jill Bolte Taylor's book, it is so empowering, what an incredible woman.

This story confirms that every interaction you have influences your energy and how you feel. These people were influencing Dr Bolte Taylor's energy with their presence, how they treated her, how they felt in her presence, the energy they took into her room depended on what they were thinking, feeling and responding to on that day. Dr Jill Bolte Taylor began to see how it was important to her own recovery to take full responsibility for protecting her own energy around other people.

It took Dr Taylor 8 years to successfully build her brain – from the inside out. Read her amazing story yourself.

11

Why Are People Vampires?

So why is it that you connect with some people, yet not with others? Why are some people positive and others negative? Why do some people have a good attitude to life and others not? Why are some people approachable and yet others are not?

In my experience I would say that there are three mains reasons. They are:

1. People Skills
2. The Grooves or Beliefs
3. Personality

People who have a different personality to yours, different grooves from yours, different belief systems to yours, these people are not good or bad, right or wrong; they are just different to you. You are different to them. You have a different life experience from them. You are totally unique and so are they. Everyone is different, with their own personality, their own reasons for believing what they believe and their own individual ability to communicate with other people. I will go on and talk more about this in the next chapter.

Depending on the above and on their "Circle of Energy", the factors that have influenced their life in the past, making them who they are today, along with the factors that are influencing their life right now (which you are probably not aware of) all of this has an influence on how people feel about themselves and their life right now, today.

It all comes down to what is going on in their head, and in their life. You never know what is happening in other people's life and you should never assume, because when you do that, it is making an Ass of U and Me.

Harden of Attitudes

Does it feel like some people need a check up from the neck up? When it comes to it, you may feel that some people need a personality transplant, or maybe you know a couple where one has a fantastic personality and it's a good job, because the others' personality is nonexistent and you may be unaware of what the connection is, in fact it's a good job that one has enough personality for both of them!

Vampire – Low Energy Human

Maybe this person is just really unhappy, or maybe they have got grotty grooves. You don't always know a person's background or who or what is going on in their life. What if they were from a background where they were never given any love or affection, bullied at school, didn't achieve in school, hate their job, not shown love or affection or attention, maybe their family have got done for shoplifting, maybe they have just lost someone in their family? The long and short of it is that you, just don't know what is going on or has gone on in that persons day, week, month, year or life.

Maybe he or she believes that they are worthless, useless or even hopeless, and maybe they just don't know how to connect with others; they don't know what you know.

Respond V React

If you can simply consider another possibility then it may help you to respond to that person instead of reacting. If that person's energy is low and you react, it can drain your energy. When you respond you will keep your own energy intact. In fact you might even help to boost their energy.

Remember:
Every interaction you have accumulates and affects you and your energy.

12

People Skills

Who have you come into contact with today and how did it leave you feeling? Think back over your day. Why would some people leave you feeling energised and other people have the opposite effect? Let's talk now about how to create positive interaction; these techniques are very easy, but they can be very challenging to follow through - it really depends on you and how you are feeling!

First of all, let me begin by telling you a story that will help you understand what I mean. One evening I was out at a dinner party with some friends and we were waiting on the last guest arriving. We hadn't seen one another for some time so we were having a great laugh and were all in high spirits. Then it happened - a Vampire walked in. The atmosphere changed instantly. It became very frosty. This particular Vampire was a friend of a friend whom I hadn't met before.

Vampires are often the kind of people who light up the room when they walk out! Unfortunately, the Vampire sat next to me and it was only a table of four! What happened next really began to challenge me; even although we were introduced, I might as well have been invisible. She began to talk to the others and she didn't make eye contact with me once. It was almost as if she was totally ignoring me. So when the waiter arrived to take our order, I ordered a glass of wine, which I obviously didn't pronounce properly, and then... she corrected me!

47

Well that just added insult to injury and by this time I was seething! I thought "Bitch!" I was livid; who did she think she was! Yes you can see, there and then I needed a sense of humour transplant! This kind of thing would normally not bother me I would usually laugh it off, but not this time. I just became really irritated by her.

So you can imagine that in this state my brain looked like a snow storm - I was so annoyed I couldn't think straight! I just kept focusing on her and found more and more things that annoyed me. What did I do?

Then I suddenly thought to myself, "Right Elaine, what can you do about this?" I knew if I carried on like this I wasn't going to enjoy my evening. If she is like this, that is her stuff, but if I take it on board, I am going to end up making it mine. So what did I do? I simply began to use some People Skills. People Skills are easy to use when you are feeling good, and confident, but are very challenging to use if someone is having a Vampire effect on you and draining your energy.

So I set out to deal with this Vampire and have a great night. Read on and find out what I did to turn the situation around. I will tell you how to use five simple People Skills that will help you create positive interaction and manage your energy with even the most challenging people. The first thing I did through gritted teeth was begin to talk to her about herself.

Talk to people about themselves.
When I first learned about this particular technique, I didn't realise how powerful it was until I began to practice using it. It involves using two words... no, not the two words you were thinking I might have used! They are very polite words - remember any form of negativity disrupts and jams up your own

energy. I really didn't want to waste any of my precious energy on this Vampire! Yes, I did feel like telling her she was a Vampire but I know that negative language has a detrimental effect on my body, so chose not to waste my precious energy by saying this to her.

When you start using these two simple words more regularly you will be amazed at the way people respond to you. The first time I began to use these simple techniques I honestly thought I was carrying a magic wand in my back pocket, I kept thinking "This is too simple, it can't be this easy!"

The two words are "You" and "Your". If you can cut back on using "I, me, my, mine" you will see the difference for yourself.

Everyone's favourite topic of conversation is themselves

I began by asking the Vampire "What is it you do?" She replied by saying she was a doctor. So I then said, "That must be a challenge, you must have to deal with a lot of Vampires?" She actually turned and looked at me rather puzzled. I explained how people can drain your energy. She understood what I was talking about right away. As I began to talk to her about herself, it started to fill up her energy tank, there was a change in the atmosphere between us immediately.

The eyes have it

The second thing I did was I looked at her when she was speaking. This is a very simple People Skill, but many people make the mistake of not using it. How do you feel if you are talking to someone and their eyes are elsewhere? How irritating is it when you are trying to hold a conversation with someone who is not looking at you? This can often happen with people who are task orientated; they are so focused on the task in hand that they don't look at you when you are speaking. Looking at someone makes them feel important and acknowledged.

Listen

Listening is a key skill, if you go back to the beginning, to the Vampire traits such as people who talk over the top of you, or jump in when you take a breath, are draining. Listening is one of the most challenging skills to develop. It is a human instinct to hear someone start to tell a story and to want to join in - it triggers your grooves. You want to tell your story too. Try just listening, giving that person your attention and just letting them speak.

So, I listened intently to the Vampire and gave her my full attention, without interrupting or giving her any of my stuff. People like to be listened to. It is one of the biggest compliments you can give to someone.

Names are important

There is one thing that people own, which is unique to them and something that they like the sound of. It is their own name. Finding out people's names and using it is important. Give them their title, get their name right, the spelling and the pronunciation.

When was the last time you got a communication with your name on it, and your name was spelt incorrectly. How did you feel? How do you feel when someone calls you by a different name even by accident? How do you feel when they pronounce your name wrong? Getting people name's correct and using it can be a huge source of energy - try it.

Everyone has different techniques for remembering people's name - just make sure you get it right. I remember a number of years ago when I was working in local government, I was in the canteen waiting to be served. The lady who was serving said to the guy in front of me "Right Morris, what would you like?" He answered "My name is Osten". Yes you guessed it she knew it was something to do with a car but she got it round the wrong way!

When you smile...

One of the best ways to create positive energy is the simplest in the world. In fact, it's an international greeting. If you want people to have a good time meeting you you need to have a good time meeting others and smiling is a good start.

What amazes me is that when you look in to a baby's pram, what is it that you look for? A smile of course! How great do you feel when a baby smiles at you? Just remember that adults are just grown up babies and start smiling.

The secret to smiling is to do it first, don't wait for someone else doing it, if you do, you are handing over control of the interaction to them. Make sure you smile, even before you open your mouth to say anything. Smiling releases endorphins from your brain, it gives you a "feel good factor".

I remember getting stuck in an airport car park in London with a taxi driver who had lost our ticket to exit the car park down the back of his radio; he took out a screwdriver to attempt to retrieve it. I decided to sort it out, so I took him into the office. When we arrived in the office we found the person in front us was a real awkward customer. She was making a real fuss about something. So the person behind the desk was really drained by the time he had finished with that customer. Immediately the clerk became free, I walked up to him smiling as I approached the desk, and said, "This is going to make you laugh!" After I

51

explained what had happened while smiling, he got us sorted and we got out of the car park free of charge, so you see, it pays to put a smile on your face.

Here is an easy way to remember all of the above. My name is Elaine and when I was a baby I couldn't pronounce it so I used to say it as "Lenys." It's the perfect acronym.

L Listen
E Use your eyes and look at the person who is talking
N Use people's names
Y Use you and your in conversation
S Smile.

Every interaction you have accumulates and affects your energy. Take control of your interactions today. No-one has the right to take away your energy so what are you doing about it?

The story I told you about the Vampire I had dinner with had a happy ending. The situation turned around completely and by the end of the evening she was like my new best friend.

Interesting conversationalist...
I remember a friend of mine telling me a story about the night she was called upon to attend a business function in place of her boss, who was unable to attend at the last moment.

When she arrived she was seated next to someone whom she knew was important to the function, but whom she had not met previously, and she began to wonder "What on earth have I in common with this guest, and what I can speak to him about?" Then she suddenly remembered something she had heard me say at an event previously on creating positive interaction. She began to talk to him about himself, and his family. Not only did she find it all very fascinating but at the end of the evening he said that she was "a very interesting conversationalist!" My friend had more or less listened for most of the evening. She did, indeed, create a positive interaction and wasn't stuck for something to say! Be interested not interesting.

These tools are all really simple when you are feeling good, but practice is the mother of all skills. When you begin to use these techniques for yourself you will understand what I mean and see that there really is power in positive interaction. It will help your energy and the energy of the person you are interacting with.

Don't wait for other people to manage the interaction; you are responsible for the energy that you take into each day and the energy that you take to meet each person in your day, so take control of your energy- you really can create a win win outcome.

If your energy and resilience are low, try the energy techniques that follow to help you deal with any negativity you feel.

My all time favourite book is by the master himself, Dale Carnegie. It is called "How to Win Friends and Influence People."

I first read this book back in my local government days, and used to put what I learned into practice. I was absolutely amazed at the difference in people's attitudes towards me. Try some of the techniques above, practice them yourself and see what happens.

Dale Carnegie's book really taught me so much about myself and others - read it and see what you think for yourself.

It's not just being aware of People Skills that is important, it is actually putting them to work for yourself.   Use them.   They really are the key to taking control and creating positive energy and interaction in your life, they really create a positive ripple effect.

A fabulous book on the ripple effect is "Pay It Forward" by Catherine Ryan.

Every interaction you have accumulates and affects you and your energy.

13

The Grooves in Your Brain

As I explained earlier, we all begin the same. We are born into the world and our life is an untold story. The adventures are just beginning. When you are born your life is like an unwritten book, a blank canvas waiting for you, the artist, to design it.

That is exactly how your brain works. Your brain changes every day with new experiences, it never stops changing, even as you progress in life. That is why my favourite saying is "You don't get older, you just get better!"

As your brain develops, your beliefs develop and your behaviour develops in direct response to your life experience and the interactions you have with other people. That is why today it is so important to become aware of your interactions, because as I always say, each interaction is a silent energy exchange which accumulates and can affect your life.

New experiences create new grooves
When you have a new experience it creates a chemical pathway in your brain. When you meet someone for the first time, when you try new food for the first time, when you drive a new car, use a different road - absolutely anything that you do for the first time creates a pathway in your brain. There are scientific names for these pathways, but I like to call them "Grooves."

Think of a lovely green piece of grass that hasn't been walked on yet. You decide to take a walk across this path one day and you use the same path the next day and the next; and the next, what happens to the grass? A pathway develops. That pathway may be just a trace at first, which then becomes a trail before it becomes an actual path.

It's the same in your brain; the more you do something the stronger the pathway becomes until you can actually use the path without even thinking about it, you do it on automatic pilot.

Once upon a time you were born

For now let's go back to the beginning of the story. When you were born you already knew how to breathe, cry, look for food, look for love, you were pre programmed by nature. It always amazes me to see animals being born, like foals for example, which get up and walk just after they are born! It is a spectacular sight; nature at its best.

When you are born you are surrounded by other people who already have a lot of life experience, beliefs, habits, etc. Why? Because, they too, are like you and have always been around other people and picked up information since the day that they were born.

Your little brain is just in the first stages of development and absorbs absolutely everything; children mimic the adults who surround them. If you are born in France to French parents you will grow up speaking French whereas if you are born in the USA you will grow up with an American accent, I was born in Scotland and I speak with a Scottish accent.

Children are not born with a favourite colour, football team, music, liking chocolate, etc, it is all part of their development and what they see, hear and experience from people around them.

Children grow grooves by listening to us

I remember one day being out for dinner with friends at a local hotel. The table we were sitting at had no outside view so I wasn't aware that it had been raining. I got up to go to the ladies room and had to pass the front door and as I did a little boy came in with his dad, and he was absolutely soaked. I said to him, "Oh my goodness look at you, you are soaked through." Now this little boy must have been around 5 years old and he looked directly at me and said "Well, that's Scottish weather for you!" I wonder where he learned to say that!

What you believe about yourself will determine what you achieve in your life, because what you believe about yourself is true for you. You do have the ability to change what you believe. First of all, it is important to become aware of what you believe and why you believe it. Is the belief you have working for you or is, in fact working against you? Is the belief about yourself or is it about others?

What do your grooves or beliefs say to you?

Let me give you an example. Many years ago I heard my mum saying something that I believed for a long time. It was the day I got my exam results, when I was 15-years-old. I remember it well - I was standing behind the sofa and as I was opening the exam result envelope, Mum was standing next to me. The paper told me I had passed all 5 of my exams, but that's all it was, just a pass and no more.

My mum was telling me that this was good. I was disappointed as my friend had got her results earlier that day, with the post being different where she lived. When I told my mum that my

friend had done much better and got different passes to me, here
is what mum replied, "Aye hen, but her parents were clever!"

Here is what I heard from that statement; "Your dad and I
weren't clever so you won't be."

In my mind I perceived you were either born clever or you were
not. So there and then I thought that I wouldn't be able to go to
university or college because I wasn't clever enough. I carried
that belief with me for a long time. So after that, if I heard
anyone mention further education I used to just think, "That's
not for me I am not clever enough."

Did I go to university and college later in life? Yes, but it was
much later in adulthood. I believed for a long time that I was
not clever enough, although one of my sister's went on to
college after school, she lived in the same house as me. She had
not heard what I heard, so she didn't have the belief that she
wasn't clever enough.

I had a groove in my brain that said "Elaine you are just not
clever enough."

Whose fault was it? It was no one's fault; my mum is one of the
most creative people I know and was simply trying to make me
feel better, and she was doing the best she knew how at the time.
I took what she said on that day and I just kept repeating it in my
head at the mention of further education. I was on automatic
when it came to it, I automatically thought "That's not for me."
It was a groove in my brain - that was what I had written on my
wall of life.

Do you go out in the morning without putting your clothes on;
do you go out without brushing your teeth? No! Why not?

You have a groove in your brain that says when you get up you brush your teeth and put on your clothes. This is what you have been taught to do by the people around you, so you do it automatically now.

If you had been born in a country where they don't wear clothes and don't have tooth brushes you would be following a different daily ritual. It is the people in your life that teach you these behaviours; rituals that give you the information to help you conform to this society.

What have the people in your life taught you to believe about who you are? What have you taught yourself to believe? Every day you are consistently consulting the grooves in your brain.

What is written there is not good or bad, right or wrong, it is just different to what is written in other people's grooves. The way we respond to life and the way we behave depend on the grooves we have in our brain.

Are you on Automatic Pilot?
When you act on automatic pilot, you are responding in the way you have been conditioned through your grooves. When you work with awareness you can change the automatic pilot programme. Is your automatic programme energising or draining?

How are you?
When someone asks you how you are, what is your usual reply? How do you normally greet others, how do you answer the telephone? If you just consider these simple questions, you will see that the reply comes to you instinctively on automatic, without giving it a second thought, as the answers are probably what you always say and have always said.

59

I used to pick up the telephone and just say "Hello." Then I made a decision that I actually wanted people to know that I was glad to hear their voice so I decided to change the way I answered the telephone. So when I get a call today, I now say "Hello Elaine speaking" with a smile in my voice. Was that easy to do? No! In the beginning I felt a bit stupid and very uncomfortable, as I was creating a new groove in my brain, and let me tell you I got some strange comments from people who knew me. But hey, that was just their stuff! Now I find it strange to answer the telephone any other way.

14

Feeding Your Brain

When you look back at the "CheerLeaders and Vampires Circle of Energy" that we talked about earlier, you can see that there are many things that influence your energy. I believe that the two things that can influence your energy more than anything are indeed, thinking and other people.

CheerLeaders are people you feel energised around, Vampires are those who you feel drained around. Do you feel energised around people who moan about this and complain about that? No, people who constantly moan can have a really negative affect and cause a multiple pile up in your energy system, if you are exposed to them regularly.

Begin to become aware of what you are consistently saying when you speak. If you know that people who moan and complain drain you, have you ever listened to your own self talk? Begin to listen to what you say to yourself in your mind. Become your biggest energiser. Give yourself encouragement. As humans we are really good at criticising ourselves. Stop draining your own energy.

Your brain listens to everything you tell it. When someone asks you how you are, what do you say? Are you "Fine", "Not Bad" or are you "Great" "Brilliant" "Excellent?" It's your choice, no one else is responsible for making you have a good or bad day, and you choose how and whether you respond or react.

Remember it's your energy and your energy is your responsibility.

I remember answering the phone one day to a friend who was having a less than perfect day. When she asked "How are you?" and I answered, "I'm great thanks." She responded by saying "Why can't you just have a crap day like everyone else?" I just laughed, that was definitely her stuff!

Just imagine waking up in the morning next to someone who moans and complains, criticising you from the moment you open your eyes. Surely you wouldn't tolerate it, so why do you do it to yourself?

I remember delivering CheerLeaders and Vampires to a group of women one morning. This is one of the questions I ask, though on this occasion I only got as far as "What would happen if you woke up one morning and there was someone in your bed who..." and before I could say anymore, an older woman in the front row shouted out..."Hen, I wouldn't get up!" Needless to say the laughter in the room really lifted everyone's energy instantly!

How do you greet people? My husband and I were travelling to the coast one morning as I was being interviewed on local radio. That morning it was raining, he went into the shop and the assistant greeted him by talking about how bad the weather was. Then she asked my husband Derek, "Where are you off to?" When he told her we were heading to the coast she replied "Oh No! The weather has to be worse over there!" He got back into the car laughing and said there was a Vampire in that shop!

When someone comments on the weather being bad I choose to respond by saying "Yes it's incredible isn't it." I choose the words I use and so can you. Someone with a great attitude is Scotland's own Billy Connolly. Billy declares that "There is no such thing as bad weather, there are only the wrong clothes!"

In the early days after working with Jack Black, of MindStore, reading my books on the use of positive language and about the effects of language on the brain, I began to change my language.

Since adopting more positive language, I never use the word "problem"; I always replace it with the word "challenge" and even to this day I find that if I do hear someone using this word, it is like a red flashing light to me.

However, creating a new groove in my brain with this word was a challenge in itself. I remember the first time I used the word in a meeting with my boss, and she just laughed at me. I felt really silly. She asked why I was using this word and I proceeded to give her the explanation. Well you may be surprised to hear that at the beginning of the meeting she had problems but by the end, they had indeed turned to challenges!

So, you see, interaction influences others. Today it is amazing the number of people in my life who use the word "challenge" now instead of "problem." Behaviour does breed behaviour. So the language you use not only feeds your brain but it also feeds your own energy and that of other people. The thoughts you have in your own mind have a direct impact on your energy. Choose your words and thoughts carefully.

15

What are People Writing on Your Wall?

I want to share something with you now that I learned from a great man called Gary Craig, who is the founder of the Emotional Freedom Technique, I will talk to you more about this later in the book.

I was watching a DVD of Gary Craig's one day when he started to talk about "The Writing on the Wall." Gary began by explaining that we all live in a palace, a palace that he calls "The Palace of Possibility." Now, within that palace we each have a room, but each of our rooms are completely different. His room is different to my room. My room is different to your room. Your room is different to the President's room, the President's room is different to my Grannie's room. All our rooms are different; the thing that makes each of the rooms different are the walls and what is written on the walls.

Do you know the song "Old MacDonald Had a Farm, E I E I O?" If you are, like me, and the majority of people I meet at my events, you will know that wee song. Who taught it to you? When did you learn it? Yes, I am sure it was a long time ago, before school or at nursery or in the early days at home. If you don't know the song, just think of a nursery rhyme you were taught a long time ago by your parents, or carer or teacher. This wee song is just something that you happen to know. It doesn't do you any harm at all knowing it. It is information that you hold in your brain or Satellite Navigation System as I sometimes call it. This wee song is written on the walls.

64

We all have different things written on our walls, and the deeper they are ingrained, the deeper the grooves are in our mind. As you are aware, I wrote on my own wall that I wasn't born clever. You can hear what is written on people's walls by listening to them speak. You will hear people say things like "I am terrible with names", "I get more forgetful as I get older", "I am too young or old to do that."

Take a young child for example; if a young child has a wee accident and drops a container of juice, he or she might be told at that time, "You are really clumsy." That might be a throw-away comment from an adult. However, the next time it happens they themselves might think, "I am clumsy." Now, the more this happens the writing on the wall might start off in pencil and, within a short time, might be written in indelible ink and then carved in stone in deep grooves. So they may grow up believing that they are clumsy. You see - every interaction you have with others does accumulate. Are you allowing people to write on your walls? What are they writing? Have you ever thought about what you might be writing on the walls of others? Do you acknowledge and appreciate people when you notice something good about them, or are you too busy highlighting or looking for what could be better, or what is wrong? Every day in every way your walls are there being written on.

The adverts you see on TV, for example. You might remember this one. "A Mars a day helps you work, rest and play". These are repeated and repeated and you hear them so often you automatically know them. Advertising does work; my question to you is what are you advertising to yourself daily, what are you saying to yourself, I can or I can't?

I remember talking to a group about "the writing on their walls" one evening and the next week a very good friend of mine came back into the group and said; "You know Elaine, I went home and had a look at the writing on my wall and I realised that it was covered in graffiti, so now I am going to get it all cleaned up and create a completely new wall."

Another fantastic friend and mentor of mine Emma Bell, who is a huge inspiration, one amazing woman, I am so grateful to have Emma in my life. When Emma heard this story about "the writing on the wall" she suggested that you create your own wall, on your laptop or in a room in your house, and put the things on it that you would like to have written on your wall, so you can physically advertise to yourself about yourself every time you see your wall.

Wendy Scott, who is a very talented writer, is a huge CheerLeader in my life. It was Wendy who told me that I help people get "The Feel Good Factor." It is thanks to the people in my life, like Wendy, and others that I mention, that you are holding this book in your hand today. They have all helped me put good grooves in my brain, by writing words of encouragement or "Words of Life" on my wall.

It's your wall, what are you going to do with it? Think about what you write on other people's walls too. Everyone needs great writing and good grooves, not graffiti or grotty grooves.

Every interaction you have accumulates and it might even end up on your wall!

16

Personality Vampires

So, let us get back once again to this important question. Why is it you connect with some people and not others? I believe one of the reasons is to do with your personality. Would you agree in life some people are outgoing, while others are more reserved? Also in life there are people who are more "people orientated" and others who are more "task orientated." This is a very simple example; if someone came to visit me at home and I was doing the ironing (which is very rare), I would stop what I was doing, make a cup of tea, and sit down and chat to them. On the other hand I have a friend who, if you visited her when she was ironing (a regular occurrence), she will get you to make the tea, and carry on with what she is doing!

Now, in the past I may have looked on a situation like that as "She is too busy, she doesn't want me here, I am in the way, I better not stay" (I was a "people pleaser" type, always putting others before myself). That is, until I came to understand that my friend was more "task orientated". These people, when they have something to do, get it done, no matter what you think, they focus on the task in hand. I am people orientated, so my focus tends to be the person and how they are feeling.

I learned this from reading various books, I recommend Positive Personality Profiles written by Dr Robert A. Rohm Ph.D; a modern approach that is easy to understand. The Great Connection by Arnie Warren, who explains the different personality types in a story and Personality Plus by Florence

Littauer who actually includes a brilliant questionnaire at the beginning of the book to help you work out your own personality style, and it helps you look at the percentage of each of the four personality types you have in you.

If I was to ask you to describe yourself, now don't think about this too much, just answer. Would you describe yourself as outgoing or reserved? What if I asked you, "Are you more people orientated or more task orientated?" What would your answer be? Here is a brief outline of Dr Rohm's theory. I would urge you to read his book. It will help you understand yourself and others better, which will help you to manage your energy better. It really can help you to keep your energy intact when you can begin to understand things from the other person's perspective.

Outgoing and Task – The Dominant Personality
People who are outgoing and task orientated tend to be relatively dominant in nature. If they want something done they may get someone else to do it; they are very determined, decisive and they get things done. They can be blunt, confrontational, and may be more difficult listeners.

I used to manage a team of people and there was a dominant type in my team I was his boss, but you would actually have got the impression that he was the boss. I am "outgoing and people" (my husband calls me "a bit scatty"). I used to hate going to work; it was like walking on eggshells - if he was having a bad day everyone knew about it!

Outgoing and People – The Inspirational Personality
People who are outgoing and people orientated are described as inspirational. They like to be the centre of attention. They are interested in people, and fun is their middle name. They are

68

very animated, enthusiastic and they talk a lot. The challenge is that they often have difficulty focusing; they avoid confrontation at all costs, and they often have to take their foot off the exaggerator. On visiting Disneyland USA with my "attention to detail" husband, I just wanted to get in there and have fun but no, he had to buy a map and plan the route! Draining or what!

Reserved and Task –The Conscientious Personality

This type of person is very information orientated. Attention to detail is important to them. They need things to be accurate. My husband has a lot of this in his personality. When I ask him to hang a picture he gets out his inch tape and begins to measure the height and width of the wall so that he gets it all precise, whereas, I would look at the wall, have a guess and get the hammer out.

If we are researching holidays on line for example, putting something through the search engine, he gets exasperated with me. When the search engine pulls up all the info, I click into this one then that one, he will say in an exasperated voice "Elaine will you please just start at the top and work your way down!" Am I draining him or what?

This type of person can often look very serious. In fact, I have heard it say that even when they are happy you wouldn't know it, because they don't tell their face. This can be quite daunting if you have to speak to a group of people with this kind of personality, you don't know whether you are making a connection or not, because their expression just doesn't give you any clues. Until I understood this I would find public speaking really daunting. Now I just love it because the personality books which explain the traits in great detail really helped me to appreciate the different characters in my audience. Not

69

everyone is expressive or animated and that doesn't mean they are not interested.

Reserved and People – The Supportive Personality

These people are very supportive and reliable. They are also relationship orientated; if you invite this person to your party he will happily chat to people if they approach him, but wouldn't dream of making the first move they are very patient people who like consistency. They have challenges with change and can be very sensitive and indecisive. My husband has a good bit of this in his personality and sometimes it drives me mad. Simple things like "Do you want a cup of tea" will be answered with "I don't know" "Do you want a cup"! "Are you hungry?" The reply would be "Are you?" Agh!

None of the above are good or bad, right or wrong, they are all just different!

Vampire Affect

So when you look at the above, very simple examples, you can see that different personalities coming together can be very draining. Dr Robert Rohm P.H.D. suggests that in the animal kingdom you wouldn't approach a lion in the same way as you would a deer. He explains that you approach animals differently based on what you know about them. And says that the same is true with people; you need to treat them based on how they are wired.

The information on personalities is so valuable because the ability to manage your energy and connect with others is so much easier when you accept that everyone has their own unique personality that is completely different to yours.

Dr Robert Rohm's book really helped me to understand myself and other people so much better. The more you understand, the more awareness you have, the better your ability to connect with other people and manage your energy in the process.

Your personality can be different depending on how you are feeling, what is happening in your life, who you are around, and what is influencing your energy. The more relaxed and at ease you are, the more your personality shines through. It can also become easier to connect with people when you begin to understand what part personality plays and accept that everyone has their own unique personality and their own way of looking at things. So the next time you come across someone who has a draining affect on you, ask yourself this; what kind of personality do they have? And remember, it's just different to yours. Or better still, feed your brain with the books I have recommended above, just like I did, you will then have your own understanding of the personalities.

It was actually Hippocrates, who is known as "The Father of Medicine", who first became aware of the four personality styles in 460 BC.

In actual fact, we all display different personalities with different people and life situations. When we are around the CheerLeaders in our life, our true self shines through and we are at ease, but when we are around draining people, events or situations, the ineffective traits of our personality raise their head.

That is why being aware of your personality and the ineffective traits can help you to work on them and, therefore, work on managing your own energy and interaction.

17

It's Just the Stuff of Life

Are people born Vampires? Are people born CheerLeaders? This is a good question to start with. When you are born, you learn to walk and talk. You do know how to cry, look for food and love. So, over the course of your life you grow from a baby into an adult and, somehow or other, through life experience, which I call "the stuff" and through being around people, you learn different behaviour. You practice the behaviour so often that it comes naturally. You behave in a certain way without even trying. You do what comes naturally, what you have been taught or what you have seen others doing or heard them saying. Very young children copy what their parents say and do. They mimic their behaviour.

All of the children in our family have their favourite football teams. Some of them could say the name of the team before they even knew what football was. They were dressed in football strips and colours and so they learned from their parents what was the best team to support. At this time they would not question anything; children accept what you tell them. At this time of your life your walls are being written on by other people all the time. At one time, everyone believed in Santa Claus – yes, I still do!

This is what happens in life; as we go we pick up other people's language, thoughts, beliefs and we have our own life experience, and it is what I like to call "The Stuff of Life."

You do not have the ability to change people's behaviour or make people see or think the way that you do by mirroring their behaviour or being forceful. If you do that you will end up draining your own energy and being your own biggest Vampire! Remember, you don't know what they have written on their wall, or what is going on in their "Circle of Energy."

Use this thought:

"It's just their stuff"

For example, driving into Edinburgh one morning I was heading towards a roundabout. I pulled into a lane in front of someone by mistake and the person behind me leaned on his horn. Previously, I would have reacted to that situation without thinking about it, and would have ended up angry and any passengers in my car would have felt uncomfortable or awkward at my outburst.

Then one day I realised: why should I get angry. If I wave and apologise and admit my error, okay I made a mistake but if he blasts his horn that is "his stuff". Why should I get angry too? I am not taking it into my day with me. Now I just tell myself someone is having a bad day! That's his stuff! He can keep it. I am not taking it with me; chances are if I take on his anger I will end up passing it onto someone else further along the road! How many times have you done that?

Other people are not right or wrong or good or bad. They are just different to you. They see the world differently to you. They know differently to you. They have different personalities from you. They have just learned to be this way. They have practiced this kind of behaviour for such a long time, and they are experts at it, probably oblivious to living in automatic pilot.

It's just their grooves at work! The way people habitually think and act establishes deep grooves in their brain.

Some people carry a lot of negative attitudes and energy around with them all the time because they have learned to do so. They don't know how to or even that they can put it down. Are you one of them?

Next time you see someone who you feel drained around just imagine that they are carrying "their stuff" or "luggage of life" around and that they are coming towards you and attempting to dump it on you. They dump a case in front of you and expect you to pick it up and carry it. When you imagine it like that you realise that in life we all have our own "stuff" and you have no reason to pick up anyone else's and carry that around too.

Use this coping mechanism to manage your emotions and interactions in a more positive way because when you are around people like this the way the interaction goes affects you, how you see it and how you respond to it affects you. If you remember "It's just their stuff" or "people's grooves" in action, it will help you to understand them better.

If you yourself are having a stressful or emotional day you may find it difficult to take a different approach and you may react negatively depending on how you are feeling. Later on I will give you a very simple technique that you can use to deal with this kind of situation, to reduce the intensity of negative emotion that you may be feeling so that you do not take it forward into your day.

I have heard it said; "Getting angry is like eating poison and expecting someone else to die" the only energy getting drained is yours.

Well Meaning Negativity?

Do other people give you their well-meaning negativity? If they do it might be your own fault. Let me give you an example of how it is really easy to collect other people's stuff without even trying.

Have you ever gone to a really busy shopping centre where there are fewer spaces than there are cars? You suddenly spot someone coming out of a space so you position yourself ready to drive in, put your indicator on and then just wait for the car to drive out. Yes and you guessed it, just as the car leaves the space free, someone else zooms into your space! You are furious. (Try being a bit peeved instead in future and see what happens.)

So you are really angry. You can't stop thinking about what happened. In fact, for the rest of the day when you meet people you know you give them a detailed explanation of what happened and then tell them how angry you are.

What happens next? You have triggered "their stuff", their "grooves", or "the writing on their wall" and they proceed to share their story with you to make you feel better so you know you are not the only one to have had this experience. They give you their well-meaning negativity. Just remember that you started it. You gave them your stuff and then you got theirs too. So by the end of the day how much of other people's stuff have you collected? So think twice in future about giving people your stuff, if you don't want theirs!

Every interaction you have affects your energy. There is always an energy exchange going on silent or otherwise. You are responsible for the energy you take to each new day, each person and situation. Take responsibility for your own energy.

Every single interaction you have with others accumulates and profoundly affects your life.

18

The Story So Far...

When I came up with the CheerLeader and Vampire theory and my observations on why people connected or not, I used to go out and do a lot of sessions, talks and events on the subject. The evaluations I received were always very positive. The testimonials I would get were very encouraging. They would always say that people really got a lot from the event, how listening to what I had to say really made them understand themselves and others better. It also inspired a lot of people to be open-minded and start reading up on the subjects I chatted about.

As you know already, I believe that the main reasons people connect or disconnect are down to:

1. People Skills
2. The Grooves, beliefs or The Writing on the Wall
3. Personality

When I did the talks to begin with, I had not yet developed "The CheerLeaders and Vampires Circle of Energy."

So when I went out to talk to people about managing negativity, the key areas that I would talk about were becoming more aware of the people skills you have, and using them. I would talk about how people got their beliefs from "The Writing on the Wall", and how these developed into "grooves", or habits of thinking and habits of behaviour. I would explain briefly about the different personality styles I had read about from the experts in the books I have told you about earlier in this book. So all of this information is great and goes down really well. However, that is just the story so far.

Something missing

The people who attended my talks were very supportive of "CheerLeaders and Vampires" because they understood exactly what I was talking about, but sometimes I used to become very frustrated and a bit defensive. Occasionally, if I was working with a small group and we were talking about the Vampires, sometimes people would say to me, "Yes Elaine, I understand what you mean, and I understand that my Vampire has a different personality from me and different beliefs from me, but even if I try and appreciate that and even if I try and use the people skills you have told me about, it really doesn't change the way I FEEL about this person."

Now, in those days before I did more work on feelings, energy and emotion, I would just put it down to the fact that these people were not ready or willing to move forward and let the past go.

I have always had excellent feedback on CheerLeaders and Vampires, how using "People Skills", or using the thought "It's just their stuff", understanding personalities helped people not to be as judgemental with their bosses or customers and they used more patience and empathy. Also understanding "The Writing on the Wall" and "The Grooves" in the brain, helped people realise what they were writing on their own wall, and the walls of other people with the language they used and comments they made from day to day.

But even with my own experience, I too, sometimes found it impossible to use my own tools in interaction, because no matter what I did I just could not change the way I felt about particular people who really challenged me. So I knew deep down that there had to be something else - but what was it? There was something missing, but I didn't know what it was. Then it happened. I found it, or rather it found me! So now I want to take things a step further and help you understand why...

...every single interaction you have accumulates and profoundly affects your energy and your life.

19

Where Do You Feel It?

So for now let us take a step back. When I spoke to you about CheerLeaders and Vampires in the beginning of the book I asked you this question "Who have you come into contact with today and how did it leave you feeling energised or drained?"

How do you know someone is having a Vampire, draining, irritating, or annoying affect on you? You just know, because you can sense it. You feeeeeeel it immediately. Instinctively you just know. It doesn't take you half an hour to have an instinct. It is instant.

This is very important I will say it again - you can feel it. You don't always see it or hear it, but you can always tell by the feeling you get. In some instances, you don't need to be in the same room. The person can be on the phone, or you can be having a conversation with someone and even when the person's name comes up in conversation, you get that same old gut feeling. When the very thought of that person enters your head, it can conjure up particular feelings that leave you feeling less than great.

Alarm bells...
It is your brain or, as I call it, your "Satellite Navigation System" (which I call your Sat Nav for short), transmitting information to you. There may be alarm bells sounding and red lights flashing in your head when you are around or think of the

Vampire! You just get a feeling. What is that feeling? It is your energy. Energy is instant!

Your body is an amazing piece of equipment; it is biological in nature and also energetic in nature. Your body is sending electrical messages around and through it constantly, these messages originate from your brain or your Sat Nav system.

Every time you have a Vampire present, or you become your own Vampire by entertaining negative thoughts, feelings or emotions, your energy gets stuck. How do you know it is stuck?

Imagine your body's energy like a motorway of traffic flowing freely. When someone causes an obstruction it has an impact on the rest of the traffic, and slows everything up; sometimes things even come to a standstill.

The same thing happens in your body. When you experience a Vampire or negative thought, feeling or emotion, it traps the energy in your body, and you feel it instantly. Maybe it's in your stomach, the way it turns, or maybe you develop a brick in it! You might feel it in the way your skin begins to crawl. You may feel it in the way the hairs on the back of your neck stand up, or the tension in your shoulders, or the way your heart sinks.

All negative or Vampire emotions disrupt your body's energy system, causing a traffic jam slowing you up and draining your energy tank and you feel it instantly. If you don't release it and get it moving again, it can cause a multiple pile up! You can lose the connection to your Sat Nav and feel like you don't know how to get out of it or move forward, leaving you feeling zapped of energy, irritable, headachy, stressed, confused, upset, and tired or in extreme cases in ill health. Shortly, I am going to explain to you how to deal with the traffic jam.

Your Own Satellite Navigation System

Your brain and your body are incredible - they are more amazing than the most advanced computer in the world. Your mind and body are bubbling with energy as you are already aware. You feel the effects of that energy moment to moment when you are around other people. You feel energised around some people and drained around others as we have already discussed. If you are consistently feeding yourself with negative thinking and self talk then you are having a Vampire effect on your own energy.

When you experience negative energy it disrupts you emotionally. This negative energy can have an adverse effect on you and on your day. When you come into contact with someone or something early in your day, someone who has irritated, annoyed, frustrated you, or a situation that is troubling you, you may go through your day without verbalising it to anyone else, keeping your stuff to yourself. This is admirable, not giving it to anyone and everyone else, but what is the feeling doing to you underneath. It may be disrupting how you feel, your ability to concentrate or even communicate.

What if this has happened earlier in your life? How long have you carried this disruptive feeling with you for? Every time you have a similar experience or any sort of reminder, up comes the feeling again. The feeling never seems to go away.

However, it may not stop you seething underneath, or even being anxious and stressed. Chances are that you may keep thinking about it, replaying it in your mind over and again, and, as you know, it drains you, disrupting your energy system. Although you haven't given anyone else "your stuff," it may not stop you being irritable towards others, and irritable in yourself.

So it is still really affecting you underneath and draining your energy for the rest of your day or even longer.

How can you stop that negative emotion going on? How can you stop yourself replaying it in your head? When you constantly replay it it can create stress in your body. Depending on what happened it may even affect your evening, and your sleep. The bottom line is the more you think about it the harder it is for you to dismiss it. It is easy for others to say "just forget it," or "think about something else, get your mind onto something else," but they are not experiencing it.

The more you think about it, the more you are deepening the groove in your brain, the more you are creating negative emotion and it's disrupting how you feel in your body.

Take bullying for example. If someone is being bullied what happens when they get home? Are the bullies still with them? Of course - they are still in the person's head. When at home, the person being bullied will consistently experience fear and worry, causing more stress and negative emotion. By tuning into the experience of being bullied, the person automatically experiences the feelings they experienced when they were actually being bullied. The repercussions of bullying can live with people for years affecting their confidence and self esteem.

The brain records the experience and the emotions associated with it. So, when you relive any experience in your mind, you will automatically relive the feelings or emotions that are attached to it in your body or energy system. I think of the brain like a satellite navigation system; you give it the memory and it automatically takes you through the experience. You give a satellite navigation system the destination and it automatically takes you there.

My husband bought me a satellite navigation system for my Christmas. I remember tapping in a destination one day when I was at home and I opened the back door so it could connect to the satellite, and get the route. I remember thinking, this is just amazing! I trusted that the woman who spoke to me from this wee box could tell me exactly how to get to my destination, even although it was not physically attached to anything I could see, but there was an energy signal being sent from the satellite to the machine in my hand. How amazing technology is.

Then I thought your brain is your satellite navigation system. You give it information and it sends energy round your body to determine how you are feeling.

Your own thinking sends electrical energetic signals around your body, in accordance with whether the thought is positive or negative, so what you choose to think or how you feel in the presence of others sends electrical signals round your body that increase or decrease your energy flow; you know this because you can feel it.

When you are constantly thinking about something or someone that has upset you in some way your brain sends signals around your body which disrupt and drain your energy.

The information which is being fed to your brain is important, as it affects you and how you are feeling. That is why awareness is one of the first keys to managing your energy because the more aware you are of negative people the more you can take control of the information which is being sent around your brain and body, and do something to deal with the negative energy that is penetrating the atmosphere.

Your satellite navigation system holds all your memories, whether they are positive or negative. It is on hand at every second to give you all the emotions that you have ever experienced. They are all just a thought away, and they are all held in your body's energetic system.

So what I began to realise was that all of the skills I was sharing were fantastic but what I really needed was to be able to help people to deal with the negative emotions and feelings that they were experiencing in their energy to deal with the Vampire feelings that were creating a traffic jam in their bodies.

20

The Rest of the Story

Then it happened! I found what I was looking for through a good friend who is a phenomenal CheerLeader in my life, but who pestered me to check out some information. First of all let me tell you the story of how we met.

I arrived in Broxburn just outside Edinburgh. I was at the Masonic Hall to do a Scottish Slimmers class. To my knowledge I was there alone, however, Rhona Hanlon turned up, unknown to me she had been the previous class manager's assistant. So we introduced ourselves then got on with the job of registering people in at the welcome table.

I got up to speak to the class. Obviously, Rhona and the rest of the members in the room had never heard me speak before. Now I love people. I tend to be somewhat animated when I speak. The people I was speaking to were more mature, and I think they were rather dazed by this strange woman who was bouncing about in front of them and talking about positive energy. The group were very receptive, if somewhat surprised. I have to say I went on to have some phenomenal people in that particular group; I just loved them, getting to know them, watching their progress, watching their appearance and confidence change. Anyway, unknown to me that day, Rhona didn't realise there had been a change of class manager and originally she turned up to hand in her notice. However, that changed and she decided to stay on and help me.

Later on as I got to know Rhona better she confessed that she had gone home to her husband that night and said "You should have seen this woman who came to take over the Broxburn Class I think she was beamed in from another planet!" She could see the look of surprise on the members' faces, and she herself was a bit taken aback, but the great thing was she stayed with me and I am so glad that she did.

Rhona was my assistant in lots of the classes that I took so she was constantly hearing me talking about energy and getting "The Feel Good Factor." Rhona also attended the early CheerLeader and Vampire talks I did and understood my work. One day I was with her and she started to talk about something that she called "Tapping." She was really enthusiastic about it and kept telling me that this is what I had been looking for. I was sceptical, although I did listen.

This "Tapping" thing that she spoke about seemed very simple. It just involved gently tapping certain energy points on the body while thinking about whatever is troubling you or disrupting your energy at the time. This tapping action calms the Vampire energy or disruption and dissolves the intensity of the negative emotion in the body. I was still sceptical, to me it all sounded just too simple.

Rhona had invested in a home study course. She was so intrigued by the success of this "Tapping"; it had helped her deal with the extreme back pain that she had suffered from for many years. It was also helping her with her low mood or depression that she had been suffering for some time. Obviously, these were major things in Rhona's life that had really affected her energy and her quality of life.

Rhona suggested that I download the free "Tapping" manual from the website and read it for myself. Yes, I downloaded it and began to read about it, but Rhona was getting impatient with me and eventually handed me a DVD telling me to take it away and watch it. I did what she said. I watched it. As soon as I watched it, I just got it. I knew right away it was what I had been looking for but I was still sceptical; it just seemed so simple.

What I had found is something known as Emotional Freedom Technique (EFT) but is more affectionately known as "Tapping." It was founded by a Harvard Engineer called Gary Craig. I spoke about Gary earlier in the book; it was Gary who introduced me to "The Writing on the Wall" idea.

The Tapping Technique is very simple and I tried it out on myself. I would use it when I became frustrated with people or if I was worried about something. I tried it out on lots of things that drained me. I was really surprised how easy it was and how quickly it seemed to work but I was still sceptical. I just kept thinking how can something that is so easy to do be so effective? It certainly worked though. I used it when I had been around Vampires, if I was irritated, upset or drained. It really gave my energy and my confidence a boost. I would use it if I knew I was going to be around Vampires. Somehow, it just seemed to change the way I felt around them and helped me stay much calmer and more relaxed.

I used to try it out on anything and everything when I felt my energy being challenged, drained or disrupted. One day I was asked to help a young boy who had a fear of going upstairs by himself in the day time; he always needed to know his grannie was waiting for him at the bottom of the stairs. Again, I didn't know what would happen, and I only had five minutes to work with him so I showed him how to do the Tapping. Within one minute his fear seemed to disappear. I thought he was putting it on but the next week his Gran called me to say he was going up and down stairs happily by himself. I have to say although I knew this was helping I still needed more convincing.

Situations seemed to arise that gave me the opportunity to help people and I was realising just how powerful this very simple technique is. Before I give you more success stories of how this simple technique has helped my clients let me tell you that Emotional Freedom Technique (EFT) or, the tapping technique, is becoming known as probably the quickest method of stress relief there is today. That is why I share it with others; it is the one thing that really can take away that Vampire feeling that disrupts your energy.

21

Emotional Freedom Technique

The theory behind EFT is that all emotional upsets are caused by a disturbance to the body's energy system; the traffic jam affect. Tapping on the body's energy points while repeating a phrase can correct the disturbance or draining effect you experience around negativity. I have included a diagram to show you the Tapping Points.

The best way to learn Tapping (EFT –Emotional Freedom Technique) is to be taught by a real person. I demonstrate the Tapping technique when I deliver "CheerLeaders and Vampire" talks. It is very simple anyone can do it. Try it for yourself.

For more details on the procedure and more information on the psychology behind EFT and the workings of the body's energies get the original manual from the creator of EFT, Gary Craig: http://www.emofree.com/downloadeftmanual.asp

How to Tap
First of all think about who or what has drained or upset you. What emotion are you experiencing? Is it hurt, pain, anger, frustration? Whatever the emotion is that you are experiencing give it a number. Where do you feel it in your body? On a scale of 1 to 10, how intense is the feeling?

Use EFT to tap the feeling away. Focus on the feeling as you follow the instructions. It doesn't matter which hand you use or which side of the body you tap on. It is usually easier to tap with the first two fingers of your hand.

Tapping Procedure

i. Find the Karate Chop point – the point on the side of the hand where you would Karate Chop something. Tap it while repeating "Even although I have this feeling, I deeply and completely accept myself." Say this calmly and with feeling three times while tapping the Karate Chop point.

ii. Now just repeat a reminder phrase "This feeling" once for each of the following points, which you should gently tap about 7 times in a row each. Don't worry about getting the precise point, as long as you get the general area, that will be fine.

1. The top or your head

2. The eyebrow, by the bridge of your nose

3. The side of your eye

4. Under your eye

5. Under your nose

6. On your chin

7. On your collar bone

8. Under your arm

iii. Take a deep breath, relax and take a drink of water.

Now go back to the same feeling you had before. Think of the same thing or person you thought of to bring the emotion up in your body. What is intensity now? Has the feeling changed? Any change is good. It shows that the Tapping has done something. For example, you may have had an intensity of pressure or stress on your shoulder that you scored 8 and now the intensity might score 5.

You can carry on doing more rounds whilst saying "Even although I **still** have this..." or "even although I have this remaining..."

Tapping really can dissolve negative emotion or energy that is draining or disrupting your body. It is being used all over the world today for different challenges. I would encourage you to research it further for yourself. I use it daily to balance my own energy. I share it with my clients for stress relief and to aid healing.

I recommend you watch "The Tapping Solution" on DVD, to purchase this please visit www.thetappingsolution.com

Tapping Points

Top of the Head

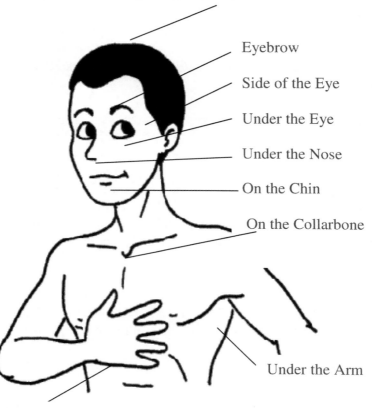

Eyebrow

Side of the Eye

Under the Eye

Under the Nose

On the Chin

On the Collarbone

Under the Arm

The Karate Chop Point

Above image courtesy Brad Yates 2004 © www.bradyates.net

The Discovery Statement

"The cause of all negative emotions is a disruption in the body's energy system."   Gary Craig

Try it on everything and anything!

22

How to Stop the Traffic Jam in Your Body

As I explained earlier, you can feel Vampire energy even when it's caused by your own thoughts. It causes a jam, block or disruption in your energetic body. Your energy just gets stuck. How do you know it is stuck? You get a feeling in your body; it drains you in some way physically and/or emotionally. It's that sinking feeling in your stomach, the tight feeling in your chest, the tension in your shoulders.

"All negative emotion is a disruption on the body's energy field." Gary Craig

The more this happens the more it affects your body, the more it disrupts how you are feeling. It can affect your attitude, your productivity, your confidence, and it lowers your resilience. This is demonstrated in "The CheerLeaders and Vampires Circle of Energy" on page 32. If this is happening often, you may become uptight, irritated, tired, stressed and in some cases severe stress can lead to ill health.

Emotional Freedom Technique (EFT) or Tapping

Emotion: another word for energy; energy in motion.
Freedom: it helps you free up the blocked energy.
Technique: is a procedure used to accomplish something.

Just like you tap a destination into a satellite navigation system and it gives you the quickest route, you tap on pressure points in your body, whilst thinking about what is irritating or stressing you. It sounds strange and I will be honest it does look a bit strange. The only way to appreciate how effective it is, is to try it. It takes you to where you want to go, a calmer place.

First of all, whom or what is causing the traffic jam? Right now think about someone who challenges you or a situation with someone that has upset you.

Let me give you a simple example; a friend of mine came to see me one evening. She is normally a very together and calm person, but that evening, right in the middle of our conversation, for no reason, she just burst into tears. I am going to call my friend Mel, to protect her identity here.

When something upsets you, you tend to think about it a lot and replay it in your mind over and over causing even more tension, disruption and upset in your body and totally draining yourself. As it plays on your mind you are being the Vampire now by playing it over and over. This is completely natural.

When I asked Mel what was wrong she told me that someone at work had really upset her that day. There was some sort of confrontation that had gone on.

So here is how I helped her overcome it; first of all I asked the Vampires' name she told me it was Helen. Then I asked "When you think of Helen what emotion do you feel?" Mel answered that she felt fear.

What is the intensity of the feeling?
When I asked Mel, on a scale of 1-10 how much fear she felt, if 10 is really scared and 1 is practically no fear at all. She answered she was at 8.

So I asked her to repeat a phrase after me. Whilst tapping the pressure points. See EFT –Tapping Points (93) for the diagram on where to tap.

The Set up Phrase

The phrase that I asked her to repeat is just called "The Setup Phrase." Here is the phrase we used.

"Even although Helen is a Vampire I accept myself anyway".

While tapping the Karate Chop point (on the side of the hand) we repeated this set up phrase three times.

What this does is it helps you to acknowledge how you are feeling instead of suppressing it.

Then we moved on to dealing with disruption; the negative energy that Mel was experiencing when she thought about this situation.

The Reminder Phrase

We tapped round the eight pressure points or energy points on the body repeating what we call "The Reminder Phrase."

The reminder phrase that we used was "Helen is a Vampire."

After doing this I asked Mel how she was feeling now when she thought about Helen. She said that the intensity of the fear feeling had gone down to a 5. So, once again, we performed the Setup phrase;

"Even although I **still** have some fear when I think of Helen I accept myself anyway.

Then we tapped on the rest of the points again using "The Reminder Phrase", which was "This remaining fear with Helen."

After doing this I asked Mel what she was feeling now. She said that the fear feeling had gone down to a 5, but that she felt annoyed at herself for feeling afraid.

So this is what we did next.
The Setup was "Even although I am annoyed at myself for being afraid of Helen, I accept myself anyway."

Then we did the Reminder tapping "I am annoyed at myself for being afraid of Helen."

After a couple of rounds the intensity of the negative feeling, had gone down to a 2. So we got the traffic flowing again Mel felt so much calmer and in control.

The next day when she went to work she felt much more in control and didn't get drained when Helen was around. She felt a little discomfort so she went to the toilet and did another couple of rounds of tapping for what she was feeling and her day went great.

If you think of someone who has upset you and specifically what it was that upset you, you can try this out for yourself. Take responsibility for what you are tapping for.
This technique is very powerful and can be used in the moment that you are experiencing the disruptive emotion, or as close to the moment as is possible, when it is appropriate to do so. I have shown you a very simple example of how you can begin to use this technique to manage your daily interactions. Try tapping for what is worrying you before you go into your day, or

before you go to bed in the evening, to help you get a good night's sleep.

For example;
While tapping the Karate Chop you might say something like;

"Even although I am worried about this meeting with John I accept myself anyway." (repeat this phrase three times)

Then tap the energy points on the body and repeat the middle part, known as, "The Reminder Phrase."

"I am worried about this meeting with John."

As you tap, you may have other thoughts, or feelings that come into your mind as a result of the tapping. This is your mind giving you information on the root of what is upsetting you, so carry on tapping for what comes up.

Emotional Freedom Techniques (EFT) is used by several million people worldwide, including therapists, nurses and doctors, teachers. It is the probably the most popular form of Energy Psychology. To appreciate the extent of its use please visit www.emofree.com and find out for yourself.

23

A Little Bit of Background

I just want to give you a little bit of my own background. I am very passionate about helping people manage stress in their life. Why? It was stress, overwork, being overwhelmed, overloaded, call it what you will, that caused my father to have a nervous breakdown when I was only 5-years-old.

At the time he was admitted to a psychiatric hospital and given medication. He was given drugs known as Valium and told by the doctor that he would need to take them for the rest of his life, which was big writing on his wall! These particular drugs caused dad to become claustraphobic and often gave him panic attacks. At the time we weren't really aware it was the drugs that were causing these side effects. Anyhow, my dad used alcohol to change the way he felt, which at the time (of course) we just didn't understand and we (mum and my sisters) just thought he was addicted to alcohol. So, to cut a long story short, he really wasn't around much in my younger days, it was mainly mum. It wasn't his fault.

Today my dad is one of life's CheerLeaders. He is still withdrawing very gradually from the medication, and eventually in the near future he will be free of the drugs. It is his decision and he has been working on it now, with the help of his doctor, for a long time. He uses EFT to aid him daily with the withdrawal symptoms. He spends most of his time helping other people and he helps me as much as he can in the work I do. I am proud of my dad to have come through what he did, and be the happy chappy he is today, who constantly sings "One day at a time sweet Jesus."

My mum is another great CheerLeader in my life. Today she helps me in my work, and my parents are both also involved with prescribed drug addiction organisations. Back in the early days, though, mum was very shy and retiring. She was quite a frightened person. The reason I say that is that I remember very vaguely when dad was in hospital and we were home alone, (myself, mum, my two sisters Jennifer and Maureen). At bedtime we used to all sleep in the same room with the double bed shoved up against the door, so mum knew we were safe.

High school was better than primary school; I became a little more confident then. Again during those years dad was still really ill and mum used to struggle when he did get home at night from the pub, she was tired and wanted to go to bed, but she wouldn't leave him downstairs, in case he didn't switch something off. She used to get me up out of my bed to ask my dad to go to his bed (which he usually did when I asked him). Then mum would go through her nightly ritual in the kitchen. She had a wee saying - I can still say it off by heart today. In fact, it is still written on my wall today! The backdoor's locked, the window's chubbed, the tap's off, that's off, the cookers off and the iron is off. Then she would go to the living room... the front windows are chubbed, the television is off, the lamp is off, the fire is off, then it would be the front door on her way upstairs, she would try it about three times to make sure it was locked. This was all to make sure the house was secure and we were all safe from the risk of fire, and break in. This was perfectly normal to me as mum had always done it.
To be honest that was just all the stuff of life at the time; mum and dad were doing the best they knew how in the circumstances that they had. Dad was ill, again we really didn't realise this at

the time. We thought he was fine on his tablets and that he was just a drinker. Mum was always there for us. She protected us. I left school with some qualifications but nothing good enough to further my education, which at the time I never really had the desire to do. As I said to you previously in the book, I just didn't think I had been born clever enough to go to college or university - so I got a youth training scheme with the local council.

The day I got it I remember my dad actually telling me, that this was a great opportunity. If I could get a full time job there that would be me set for life. I wrote that on my wall too, although somewhat reluctantly. At the time, I remember thinking, do I really want that? So I worked with local government from the age of 16 until I was 33.

Then things changed...
Things began to change when I was thirty. At the age of thirty, I began to read. I can't say I was great at it to start with as I considered books to be something you left behind after school. So I set myself the task of reading 15 minutes per day. At first I would clock watch, but then I began to really enjoy the books. One book that really made an impact in my life in the beginning was "Feel The Fear and Do It Anyway" by Susan Jeffers; my cousin Anne-Marie Campbell had given me the book. I remember she said "Elaine if you never read another book please read this one." I read it and I really enjoyed it, so what I did was pass it onto my mum and said just exactly what Anne-Marie had said to me; "Mum, if you never read another book please read this one." Looking back I think this was the start of something for mum too.

I was on a roll and really started to read everything that was recommended to me. It was the books that first taught me how

102

to use people skills to interact with people and what I realised was how the tools that I was using were really creating positive interaction. I enjoyed using the tools. They made me feel better in myself, and I could see others responding to me in a different way, leaving everyone feeling good. It was also through reading that I realised that I could be, do and have what I wanted in my life, no matter what had already been written on my wall, so I set about changing the grooves in my brain by simply being more aware of what I was saying and thinking, using more positive language.

Of course, studying the personalities helped me realise that I was an "I type"; a people person. It really helped me in the confidence department too, as I began to see that there were a good few "D types" in my life, who I felt drained me, but reading about them helped me appreciate that their approach was just different to mine.

Then, of course, Emotional Freedom Technique arrived in my life which really is the icing on the cake as it is the one thing I can use to help dissolve negativity. I use it daily on myself and consistently share it in my sessions and with my clients to help them too.

You see, my dad has experienced, (to put it mildly) a very challenging life. But today he and mum are just amazing; they are always busy helping others. The effects of stress resulted in dad taking medication and becoming addicted which really had an adverse effect on his life and obviously affected the family life at the time. Then when he tried to come off the medication too quickly he ended up back in hospital for quite a time and the doctors gave him 24 sessions of Electric Shock Treatment. In the end, though, the only real thing that got him back on his feet was mum's suggestion to put him back on the drugs and

103

withdraw him very slowly. Mum had done her homework. She had been researching and reading books, one of which was "Back to Life" by Pam Armstrong.

So, you can see that our family life has been affected by stress in a big way. Today my work is all about helping people manage stress, getting "The Feel Good Factor" and enjoying life.

If you want more information or assistance with prescribed drug addiction please visit:

www.bcnc.org.uk
www.thetrap.org.uk
www.aata.org.uk

24

The Stress Vampire

Stress is a major player in ill health and disease, managing your energy and your interactions on a day to day basis, using this simple tapping technique really can improve the quality of your health and your life. You can try tapping for anything. Be as specific as you can about what it is that is irritating you. Just try it and see what happens.

Right now I want you to scan your body; top of your head, your scalp, your forehead, your face, in particular your lips and cheeks, then the back of your neck, your shoulders, your chest area, down your arms, your stomach, your hips, your legs, your ankles and your feet. As you do, feel for any tightness or tension in your body. It is surprising how much tension you are holding without actually realising it.

Your body and mind perform best in a relaxed state. When you are stressed, you brain almost looks like a snow storm, and it is challenging to think straight and your body can become tense. So take a deep breath right now and relax your body, repeat it again and now just once more. Feel the difference in your body?

Let's look at the definition of stress in the dictionary:

"Stress – mental or physical tension or strain, to exert pressure on, or to emphasise."

When you experience stress, all sorts of things happen in your mind and your body. Right now, think about a situation in the past that may have challenged you, something relatively simple, nothing traumatic. As you think about that situation, scan your body what do you feel now? You will probably find that somewhere in your body there is some sort of dull feeling or tension, some people often describe it as a colourful feeling, a black feeling, or a red feeling for example.

People often use the language of colour in the description of how they are feeling "I just saw red", "It was like a red rag to a bull"and "The dark mist came down."

When you think of something that challenges you, scan your body to see where the traffic jam is occurring in your energy, where are you feeling it in your body? So, again when you think a thought, your Sat Nav immediately sends the feelings around your body that you have stored in your energy system associated with that situation; your body triggers the feeling accordingly.

In his book "The Genie in Your Genes", Dawson Church PhD describes how high stress levels actually SUCK biochemical resources from your body, which interfere with cell repair in the body and kill brain cells.

So when you are stressed there is literally a Vampire effect taking place. You are being drained of life energy. All negative emotions cause a disruption in your body's energy, whether it is negative thinking, language, situations, people or otherwise.

While you may have very little control over other people, you always have a choice with regards to the thoughts you choose to think, the language or words you choose to use. So begin to become more aware of the words you are using and the thoughts you are thinking and stop being a Vampire to yourself.

25

Raise Your Awareness

I always say, "When you are aware you are in control." Becoming aware of your interactions is the first step to managing your energy. However, make sure you become open to finding the positives, as well as finding the negatives in people.

Awareness is important. What you focus on you often find, so start looking for what is good about people and situations. A good example is when you buy a car, one that you don't think you see many of. Yet the minute you buy it, you seem to see loads of them.

People have told me on various occasions that if they have been suffering with a health challenge, maybe something that is a bit unusual, when they start to talk about it and focus on it, they then come across others who have or have had a similar issue.

Have you ever booked a holiday to somewhere that you thought was quite unusual, then before you know it, you end up speaking to lots of people who have been there or are going there?

I have spoken to you about people who you feel good around, and the other people. Now you may find that you become so much more aware of the people you are interacting with. You will find people who are energising and people who are draining. When you find the ones that are draining you can start to use the techniques in this book to help you.

108

Awareness is the first step to change. The minute you are aware of something you can become a positive influence if you choose to. Your focus is really down to you; no one else is responsible for making your day good or a bad. Whether you respond or react is entirely your choice. The energy you take into each day is your responsibility. If you are reacting you are possibly doing so on automatic pilot, but when you use awareness you can move forward and manage your interactions and your energy better.

The CheerLeader and Vampire Principles:

1. Raise Your Awareness
2. Feed Your Brain
3. Practice and Repeat

Raise your awareness of who you come into contact with regularly and how it leaves you feeling.

Every interaction you have really does affect your energy; how do you manage your energy?

Use the People Skills I spoke to you about earlier.

Become aware of the Grooves in Your Brain and what is written on your wall.

Understand that your personality is unique, it's different to that of other people.

Use Emotional Freedom Technique to dissolve any negative feelings you have.

Here are some other techniques that I choose to use to manage my energy and interactions:

The Positive Shower
When I get up in the morning, I have a shower and I like to imagine that the water that is flowing over my body runs dirty to start with taking away any negative energy from my body and then I see it becoming clear and clean.

The Sun Beam
While I am still in the shower and the water has run clean, I then imagine a huge beam of very bright sunlight coming down through my body, out the soles of my feet and rooting me in the earth, so that I feel fresh, full of energy and securely grounded.

The Glass Mirror
This is something that I learned from listening at one of my events to a lady who told me about the Glass Mirror she uses. She said: "When you are interacting with someone who you feel is draining your energy imagine there is a glass mirror in front of you. You can see them through the mirror and if they could see the mirror they would see their own reflection. Whatever is being said that is negative or draining is reflecting off the glass on the mirror, so it is not entering your body's energy system."

Physically Protecting Your Energy
If possible, cross or clasp your hands in front of you just at your groin, also cross your legs at your ankles too. This is just another way of protecting your own energy tank. Just try it!

Go on give them a try and see how you feel afterwards.

26

This is Your Life

When were you born? What is your date of birth? You know that don't you, you know when you arrived on this planet? The chances are, though, you don't know the other date, the one when you leave or you pass on.

Elaine Kennedy McIvor

Date of Birth - 25 Jan 1966

to

Date of Departure - ?

There never is, was or will be anyone quite like you! This is your life! One of my mottos in life is "Here for a good time... Not a long time." People rarely know the day the hour or the minute, or what is going to happen, or what's around the next corner. Every day, in different parts of the world, people are wiped out. Just look at the number of innocent people killed in 9/11.

NO-ONE HAS THE RIGHT TO TAKE AWAY YOUR ENERGY!

Time waits for no man. It is something that everyone owns, whether you are rich or poor, happy or sad, whoever you are, wherever you are, you have it. Some have more than others, but no-one really knows how much they own, so it is important to value the time you are given and make the most of every second of every minute of every day! In order to get the most out of yourself and your life, what you do with your time, how you spend it and who you spend it with makes an impact on the quality of your life.

Making Memories
Every day in life you make memories. What memories will you make today? We have special friends, Jimmy and Norma Turnbull, from Elgin, who we spend time with each year. We organise weekends away each year, specifically to have fun and make great memories together.

"Don't Burn Daylight"
This saying came from Dr Phil. Time is so precious. Spend your time wisely. If Derek and I have a disagreement, we sort it out and apologise as soon as we can. It is just a pact that we have, we are human the same as everyone else. We just don't like wasting precious time feeling bad.

I love this quote from Charles Tremendous Jones:

"You will be the same person in 5 years' time dependant on two things, the books you read, and the people you associate with."

Time is precious and you can change your day in a heartbeat, if you choose to, by taking control of your energy. Your energy is your responsibility.

Every single interaction you have accumulates and affects you, your energy and your life.

27

You and Other People

After reading this book about CheerLeaders & Vampires, I am sure you will be able to think of people you would know as your Vampires. Even just the thought of them makes your blood run cold and changes the way you feel, affecting your energy.

I spoke to a mum recently. She was really concerned about her young daughter who had just left school and was intially really enjoying her job, however after a few months of working next to people who she didn't feel good around, the Vampires, she ended up on medication for stress. Then she left her job. It had a ripple effect, because not only was she ill, but her mother was sick with worry.

Every interaction that you have accumulates. Other people can influence your energy and how you feel. What influence are you having on people? Do you manage your energy? Have you got good grooves, do people enjoy being around you? What grooves do you set in motion in others? Do you tell people when you appreciate them, when they do something right?

I remember working in a hotel; it was a family-run business and when you slipped up and made a mistake you would hear about it five times over. Each member of the family would tell the other who would, in turn, then come and tell you off about it. They never ever highlighted anything that you did right, always what you did wrong; needless to say the turnover of staff was high and people were totally stressed always waiting to see what they were going to get told off for next.

Let's look at the implications of running on low energy. Your energy influences your attitude, your thinking, your behaviour, your confidence, your self esteem, your ability, your output, your health, your stress levels, the way you look, the way you feel, how you see yourself, how other people see you, your reputation as a human being. So it pretty much affects everything about you and your life. The quality and value of your energy is absolutely imperative to your success in life as a human being and to your overall happiness.

All these factors are influenced by your energy so it is really important to take control of your energy. The more energy you have the better you feel. In life everyone's goal is to feel good. No-one gets up in the morning, intending to feel bad. Have you ever heard anyone say: "I had a great time feeling miserable today?" In life everyone wants to feel good about themselves. How you feel affects your energy. How you feel affects how you think, and it also works the opposite way. How you think affects how you feel.

Thinking has a huge impact on how you feel. If you are sitting there thinking about something or maybe someone who annoys you it creates negative emotion in your body, which is just another word for negative energy, causing the traffic jam. What you are doing is giving away your energy just by thinking about something or someone because it affects how you feel.

No-one has the right to take away your energy. You are in charge of your energy and who you give it to is entirely up to you.

"No one can make you feel bad without your permission."

Eleanor Roosevelt

CheerLeader Energy

The people with whom we connect are those people that we feel good around. They feed our energy. They are a source of encouragement to us. They are enthusiastic, good listeners, happy and positive people. They might wear a smile, and time flies when you are together. In general, they make a positive impact in your life; you feel important, recognised, acknowledged when you are around them.

They stand on the side lines of your life and shout encouragement to you; they are energisers. When you spend time in their company you get filled up with energy, positive energy-like radiators. They heat up the room with their presence.

One of my great friends and biggest CheerLeader's Terri Craig who is an amazing person, once referred to a CheerLeader as "A Petrol Station for Positive Energy." This phrase describes Terri perfectly. Just like your car needs to be refuelled regularly, after life's journeys you also need to keep your fuel tank full and not run on empty. When your car runs on a very low fuel supply you are draining the tank nearly dry and it can have an adverse affect on the workings of the machinery. You are just the same; when you are constantly running on low energy it can adversely affect the workings of your machinery.

Vampire Energy

When around people with whom you do not connect you might feel stressed drained of all your energy. You may feel down after being with them, ignored, belittled, intimidated, invisible. They may dump their life luggage on you.

115

There are many different kinds of people who zap your energy levels. Some people don't even realise they are zapping you as they are acting on automatic. Remember - they are different from you, they have a different life experience from you. In fact, they really may need someone like you in their life to influence them, write on their wall, and create new grooves in their brain. The more you become aware of your energy, the more aware you will be that;

Every single interaction you have accumulates and affects you, your energy and your life.

If you choose to let it!

28

A CheerLeader is...

This was the very first thing I wrote away back in the beginning. It all started at a conference in Liverpool I was at, where I had been drunk on life after a fantastic lady by the name of Sue Cappelen asked the audience: "Who are the CheerLeaders in your life?" That question has stayed with me and it is the reason for my life's work today. It all started with one question that one person asked me; that woman made a huge impact on my life. She made me stop and think. So, here is my definition of a CheerLeader:-

A CheerLeader is...

Someone who has made or makes
a positive impact on your life in some way.
A constant source of encouragement.
Someone who makes you feel special.
A good listener.
Enthusiastic.
A futurist.
Someone who doesn't tell you what to do, but helps you find the answer by just listening.
Someone you enjoy spending time with. In fact, time just disappears when you are with them.
Someone with a genuine smile on their face and in their voice.
Someone who just makes the world a better place by being in it!

My Mission

My mission in life is "To Create a Global Network of People Inspiring People." I want people to get out there and create their own network because the people who inspire you may be different from the people who inspire me. Start your own network. Here is what to do:

1. When you feel good around someone tell them.

2. Arrange to touch base with them again. You decide on the method and frequency, call, text, email, lunch, coffee, dinner, whether its weekly, monthly, whatever you feel is right.

3. Duplicate the above. Encourage other people to do the same.

I love people and I make an effort to keep in touch with people who inspire me. It must be a two way relationship give and take, not a pity party, but a meeting of minds. I choose my CheerLeaders, people who want to live life to the full and encourage others to do the same. I have a cupboard full of them. My books are huge CheerLeaders in my life. Life is for living, it really is one big adventure.

Every interaction you have accumulates and affects your life and your energy.

Start by being a CheerLeader to someone in your life today. You will be amazed at the CheerLeaders who turn up in your own life!

Your life is what you decide to make it. Decide to make it great!

This is your life build it happy.

Enjoy!

Warmly
Elaine

www.elainekennedymcivor.com
www.cheerleadersandvampires.com

Recommended Reading

Positive Personality Plus   Dr Robert Rohm

The Great Connection   Arnie Warren

Personality Plus   Florence Littauer

How to Win Friends and Influence People
      Dale Carnegie

The Power of the Subconscious Mind
      Dr Joseph Murphy

Excuse Me Your Life is Waiting Lynn Grabhorn

MindStore   Jack Black

The Secret   Rhonda Byrne

Pay It Forward   Catherine Ryan

Eat That Frog   Brian Tracy

My Stroke of Insight Dr Jill Bolte Taylor, Ph.D.

The Genie in Your Genes Dawson Church Ph.D.